D1141895

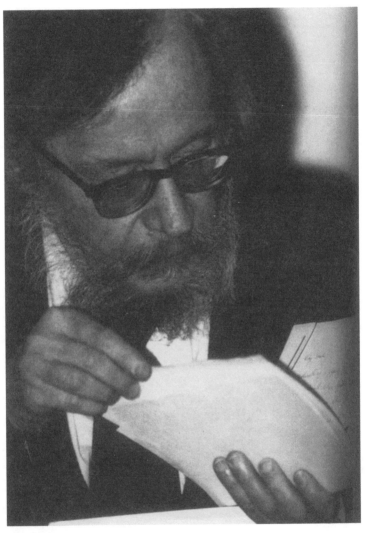

Frontispiece Jerzy Grotowski (1997). Photograph by M. Culynski

JERZY GROTOWSKI

Routledge Performance Practitioners is a series of introductory guides to the key theatre-makers of the last century. Each volume explains the background to and the work of one of the major influences on twentieth- and twenty-first-century performance.

Jerzy Grotowski was a master director, teacher and theorist whose work extends beyond the conventional limits of performance. This is the first book to combine:

- an overview of Grotowski's life and the distinct phases of his work
- an analysis of his key ideas
- a consideration of his role as director of the renowned Polish Laboratory Theatre
- a series of practical exercises offering an introduction to the principles underlying Grotowski's working methods.

As a first step towards critical understanding, and as an initial exploration before going on to further, primary research, **Routledge Performance Practitioners** are unbeatable value for today's student.

James Slowiak is Professor of Theatre at the University of Akron and co-artistic director of New World Performance Laboratory. He assisted Jerzy Grotowski in the Objective Drama Program at the University of California-Irvine and in Italy from 1983–1989.

Jairo Cuesta is co-artistic director of New World Performance Laboratory. He collaborated with Jerzy Grotowski on Theatre of Sources and the Objective Drama Program from 1976–1986.

ROUTLEDGE PERFORMANCE PRACTITIONERS

Series editor: Franc Chamberlain, University College Cork

Routledge Performance Practitioners is an innovative series of introductory handbooks on key figures in twentieth-century performance practice. Each volume focuses on a theatre-maker whose practical and theoretical work has in some way transformed the way we understand theatre and performance. The books are carefully structured to enable the reader to gain a good grasp of the fundamental elements underpinning each practitioner's work. They will provide an inspiring springboard for future study, unpacking, and explaining what can initially seem daunting.

The main sections of each book cover:

- personal biography
- explanation of key writings
- description of significant productions
- reproduction of practical exercises.

Volumes currently available in the series are:

Future volumes will include:

Antonin Artaud
Pina Bausch
Bertolt Brecht
Peter Brook
Rudolf Laban
Robert Lepage
Lee Strasberg
Mary Wigman

JERZY GROTOWSKI

*James Slowiak
and Jairo Cuesta*

Routledge
Taylor & Francis Group

LONDON AND NEW YORK

First published 2007
by Routledge
2 Park Square, Milton Park, Abingdon, Oxon OX14 4RN

Simultaneously published in the USA and Canada
by Routledge
270 Madison Ave, New York, NY 10016

*Routledge is an imprint of the Taylor & Francis Group,
an informa business*

Typeset in Perpetua by
Newgen Imaging Systems (P) Ltd, Chennai, India
Printed and bound in Great Britain by
Antony Rowe Ltd, Chippenham, Wiltshire

British Library Cataloguing in Publication Data
A catalogue record for this book is available from
the British Library

Library of Congress Cataloging in Publication Data
Slowiak, James.
    Jerzy Grotowski / by James Slowiak and Jairo Cuesta.
       p. cm.—(Routledge performance practitioners)
    Includes bibliographical references and index.
       1. Grotowski, Jerzy, 1933–1999—Criticism and interpretation.
    I. Cuesta, Jairo. II. Title.
    PN2859.P66G775 2006
    792.023'3092—dc22   2006031391

ISBN10: 0–415–25879–0 (hbk)
ISBN10: 0–415–25880–4 (pbk)
ISBN10: 0–203–96274–5 (ebk)

ISBN13: 978–0–415–25879–1 (hbk)
ISBN13: 978–0–415–25880–7 (pbk)
ISBN13: 978–0–203–96274–9 (ebk)

FOR OUR PARENTS,
RAY, YVONNE,
SABARAIN AND ALICIA

FOR KENA

AND

IN MEMORY OF BOS,
WITH DEEP GRATITUDE

CONTENTS

FIGURES

Photos 1.1–3.5 are courtesy of the Archive of the
Grotowski Centre, Wroclaw
Photos 4.1–4.4 are courtesy of New World
Performance Laboratory

ACKNOWLEDGMENTS

We would like to thank all of the current and past members of New World Performance Laboratory who have made our work possible over the years and have taught us so much, especially Debora Totti, Chris Buck, Justin Hale, Jamie Russell Hale, Megan Elk, Terence Cranendonk, Salvatore Motta, Toby Matthews, Stacey MacFarlane, Pancho Colladetti, Lisa Black, and Massoud Saidpour.

We are grateful to the theatres and festivals that have presented the work of NWPL and to the organizers and participants of the many workshops who have supported our activities while writing this book, especially Ryszard Michalski and the members of Gildia, Franco Lorenzoni and Cenci Casa-laboratorio, Kaska Seyferth and Las Teoulères, Fabio Toledi and Astragali, Ricardo Camacho and Teatro Libre, Adela Donadio and La Casa del Teatro, James Levin and Cleveland Public Theatre, Carlotta Llano, Fernando Montes, Sneja Tomassian, and Stefa Gardecka.

We are indebted to The University of Akron and Case Western Reserve University for their generous support of our teaching, research, and the writing of this book and to our many students.

We would like to thank Mark Auburn, Lisa Wolford Wylam, Chris Hariasz, and Randy Pope for useful editorial comments and Franc Chamberlain for his patience and advice.

We would like to acknowledge the directors and staff at the Centre for the Study of Jerzy Grotowski's Work and the Cultural Research in Wroclaw for their assistance throughout the writing of this book and the permission to reproduce some of the photographs contained in this volume.

We are grateful for the work and research of Zbigniew Osiński, Jennifer Kumiega, Robert Findlay, Lisa Wolford, and Eugenio Barba.

Thanks to Thomas Richards and Mario Biagini for continuing to inspire.

Special thanks to Douglas-Scott Goheen, teacher, collaborator, and friend, whose photographs grace this volume.

Our profound appreciation to Dominique Vendeville for her support and encouragement.

And finally to all of our comrades around the world who had the opportunity to travel with Grotowski on his journey: Keep the flame burning.

Every effort has been made to trace the copyright owners of the photographs used from the Grotowski Centre's and NWPL's archives. If any errors have been made in the use of such material, we will correct it in future editions. We gratefully acknowledge the following photographers: Figure 1.1, Mark E. Smith; Figure 1.5, Joanna Drankowska; Figure 3.1, Andrzej Paluchiewicz; Figure 3.3, Piotr Baracz; Figure 4.1, Marino Colucci; Figures 4.2 and 4.4, Douglas-Scott Goheen.

BIOGRAPHY AND CONTEXT

A group of excited young South American theatre artists gather at a small airport in the coffee-growing region of Colombia. It is late summer 1970. The brisk mountain air makes them shiver, adding to the tense aura of expectation. These representatives of the International Theatre Festival of Manizales, one of the oldest on the continent, await the arrival of the Festival's honorary president, Jerzy Grotowski.

Grotowski's company, the Polish Laboratory Theatre, is at the height of its fame. Paris, Edinburgh, and New York have sung Grotowski's praises, and the Latin American artists are eager to share in the euphoria of this theatre revolution. Some of them attended performances of *The Constant Prince* at the Olympic Arts Festival in Mexico City in 1968. Others have seen only photos of the company's groundbreaking productions and of the portly man in dark glasses and black business suit who directs the group. All of them have been warned of Grotowski's severity and his caustic critiques of avant-garde theatre and amateur training methods.

The group shivers again with anticipation and cold as the plane approaches. Upon landing, the door opens, and to everyone's surprise, out steps a thin, bearded wanderer, dressed in flimsy, white cotton, wearing sandals on his bare feet, and carrying a knapsack. Grotowski had transformed himself. As the shocked Colombians run to find him a woolen poncho to protect him from the chill, the theatre world holds its breath.

THE ENIGMA

Grotowski (Figure 1.1) was always an enigma. He has been called a master and a charlatan; a guru and a sage; a myth and a monster. Throughout his relatively brief career (he died at the age of 65), Grotowski went through numerous permutations, often catching his critics, and even his friends, off guard.

Figure 1.1 Jerzy Grotowski (1975). Photograph by Mark E. Smith

Spending his childhood under Nazi domination and maturing during the darkest days of Stalinism, he learned at a young age how to use the system in order to seek the best conditions for his work—and always without compromise. He knew that fame was necessary to reach his goals. He knew that fame outside his home country of Poland would be far more beneficial than fame inside Poland. But he also knew that fame was fleeting and that it would be dangerous to succumb to its intoxication.

When the time was right, Grotowski turned his back on fame. He transformed himself. He was able to do this because he always had a plan, a parallel objective to his creative work, a "hidden agenda." This hidden agenda guided many of his choices throughout his career as a stage director and even after he left the arena of public performances.

GROTOWSKI'S FORMATIVE YEARS

Jerzy Marian Grotowski was born in the small town of Rzeszow in south-eastern Poland on August 11, 1933. His mother, Emilia (1897–1978), was a schoolteacher and his father, Marian (1898–1968), worked as a forest ranger and painter. An older brother, Kazimierz, was born in 1930. When Hitler's Germany invaded Poland in September 1939, Grotowski's father escaped to France and then England, fighting as an officer in the Polish army. After the war, Marian Grotowski, a strong anti-Soviet, refused to return to Poland and immigrated to Paraguay. From the age of six, Grotowski never saw his father again. He was nourished by his mother's strength and affection.

When war broke out, Emilia Grotowska moved the family to a small village, Nienadowka, about 12 miles north of Rzeszow. Here they lived meagerly on her teacher's salary. These formative years colored many of Grotowski's perceptions and interests throughout his life. In this tiny village, among peasants, he first confronted tradition, folk beliefs, and ritual, while Grotowski's mother introduced her sons to the spectrum of religious thought.

EARLY INFLUENCES

One day Grotowski's mother brought home Paul Brunton's *A Search in Secret India*, a curious volume about an English journalist's contact with the mysteries of India. Around the same time, the village priest secretly gave the young Grotowski a copy of the Gospels to read alone. In those years, the Polish Catholic church required the presence and interpretation of a priest to read the Gospels, but Grotowski first encountered Jesus, by himself, in a hayloft above the pigpen of the farm where he lived.

These books—along with Renan's *The Life of Jesus*—plus *The Zohar*, *The Koran*, and the writings of **Martin Buber** and **Fyodor Dostoevsky**, served as the foundation for the questions Grotowski pursued during each phase of his creative investigations. But it was Brunton's book that affected Grotowski most profoundly.

Martin Buber (1878–1965): Jewish philosopher, influenced by Jewish mysticism, who believed that one's relation with God could be a direct, personal dialogue. His writings include *I and Thou* (1923), *Gog and Magog* (1953), and *Tales of the Hasidim* (1908).

Fyodor Dostoevsky (1821–81): Russian novelist. His masterpiece, *The Brothers Karamazov*, includes a parable about "The Grand Inquisitor" who arrests Jesus when he returns to earth. Grotowski included this text in his play *Apocalypsis cum figuris*.

Through Brunton's writings, Grotowski discovered the teachings of the Hindu mystic **Ramana Maharshi (1879–1950)**. Ramana Maharshi believed that a deep investigation of the question "Who-am-I?" would cause the socialized, ego-oriented, limited "I" to disappear and reveal one's true, undivided being. When pilgrims asked Ramana Maharshi to clarify the meaning of life, the wise man would respond with the statement: "Ask yourself who-am-I." The young Grotowski reacted strongly to these ideas and his pursuit of the question, *Who-am-I?* developed into one of the chief threads of his life and work.

Already at the age of 10, people with a special kind of wisdom, like Ramana Maharshi, fascinated Grotowski. Later in life, he called such people by the Russian word *yurodiviy*, "holy fool," and he dedicated one aspect of his investigation to making contact with such *yurodiviy*, directly. Actual **transmission** of knowledge, whether received or stolen, through real confrontation with a master, became a special field of interest for Grotowski. In fact, transmission became the main thrust of the last period of his work and defined his relationship with **Thomas Richards (b. 1962)**, an American actor who, since Grotowski's death, directs his research center.

THEATRE SCHOOL

In 1950, Grotowski's family moved to Krakow where he finished his secondary studies. He had missed a year of school due to illness, the beginning of serious health problems that would plague Grotowski throughout his life. Undecided as to which discipline he should choose for a career, Grotowski sent out three applications for advanced study: one to the medical school for psychiatry; one to the program in Oriental Studies; and, finally, one to the Acting Department of the State Theatre School in Krakow. The Theatre School was the first to respond and Grotowski's destiny was determined.

On the entrance exam he received only "satisfactory" grades for his practical work, including an "F" for diction. However, his essay on the topic, "How can theatre contribute to the development of socialism in Poland?" received an "A" and he was accepted into the program on probation.

Grotowski often said that theatre studies appealed to him because, although performances themselves operated under strict censure by the Polish government, rehearsals were unregulated. He believed that the rehearsal process might provide a fertile field to seek answers to his questions.

While in theatre school, Grotowski continued to develop his interest in Asia. He studied Sanskrit and met with specialists. He also published several articles forming the basis for his future theatre pronouncements: one article included a call for more government support of young theatre artists; another article envisioned a "theatre of grand emotions," in which action is structured consciously and real-life details are used only when "absolutely necessary to evoke the emotions or to clarify the action . . ." (cited in Osiński 1986: 17).

Upon graduation with an actor's certificate in June 1955, Grotowski was assigned to the Stary Theatre of Krakow. His contract was delayed, however, when he received a scholarship to study directing at the State Institute of Theatre Arts (GITIS) in Moscow.

THE RUSSIAN CONNECTION

When Grotowski left for Moscow in August 1955, he was known as a "fanatic disciple of **Stanislavsky**" (Osiński 1986: 17; emphasis mine). Stanislavsky's system was the "official" curriculum of the Polish theatre school, but most students regarded the Russian's contributions to actor training with disdain. Grotowski, however, saw the seeds of truth in Stanislavsky's **system of physical actions**, and he went to Moscow to study the system at its source.

> Russian actor and director **Konstantin Stanislavsky (1863–1938)**: established the Moscow Art Theatre with Vladimir Nemirovich-Danchenko (1858–1943) in 1898. The **system of physical actions**, one of his final innovations, highlights doing rather than emotion as the actor's fundamental tool.

During his year at GITIS, Grotowski studied with **Yuri Zavadsky (1894–1977)**. Zavadsky, an actor who had performed under Stanislavsky and **Evgeny Vakhtangov**, now directed theatre productions that followed the strict **socialist-realistic style**. Zavadsky observed that Grotowski instinctively worked with actors in a manner similar to Stanislavsky himself. One day Grotowski visited Zavadsky's apartment. The teacher showed the student his awards, his passport (unusual under Soviet socialism), and the two limousines and chauffeurs at his disposal. Zavadsky whispered, "I have lived through dreadful times and they have broken me. Remember, Jerzy: *nie warto*, it is not worth it. This is the harvest of compromise" (cited in Barba 1999: 24). Years later Grotowski revealed that this episode touched him deeply and gave him the strength to resist the pressures of compromise during his years of working under an oppressive political system. Grotowski considered Zavadsky as one of his great masters (Barba 1999: 24–5).

> **Evgeny Vakhtangov (1883–1922)**: student of Stanislavsky who directed the Moscow Art Theatre's First Studio and developed his own creative style of production called "fantastic realism." Grotowski was especially influenced by his playful production of *Turandot* (1922).

> **Socialist-realism**: was the predominant art form in the Soviet Union under the rule of Joseph Stalin (1879–1953). Its goals were to realistically and heroically depict the aspects of revolution and the common worker's life in an optimistic fashion, while educating the public in the principles of communism.

In Moscow, Grotowski also discovered the theatre experiments of Stanislavsky's protégé, **Vsevelod Meyerhold (1874–1940)**. Meyerhold's innovative staging techniques, actor-training methods, and dramaturgy led him into direct confrontation with the Soviet authorities. In 1939, he was imprisoned and then executed for his refusal to submit to the artistic homogeneity required during Stalin's regime. Meyerhold's name and contributions were erased from historical records and he had yet to be "rehabilitated" by the post-Stalin authorities during Grotowski's stay in Moscow. The curious Polish director, with the aid of a kindly librarian, would sneak into a locked section of the library after-hours and pore over the forbidden documents describing Meyerhold's ground-breaking theatre work. Grotowski said that from Stanislavsky he learned how to work with actors, but it was from Meyerhold that he discovered the creative possibilities of the stage director's craft.

FIRST TRAVELS

Upon completion of his one year of studies in Moscow, with his health in a precarious state, Grotowski embarked on a two-month trip to Central Asia (Figure 1.2). This trip, his first direct encounter with the East, further stimulated his interests in Asian philosophy and the practical aspects of Asian traditional and classic performing arts. He often spoke of a special meeting with one of the holy fools (*yurodiviy*) that occurred on this trip: "I met an old Afghan named Abdullah who performed for me a pantomime 'of the whole world', which had been a tradition in his family" (cited in Osiński 1986: 18). Grotowski saw his own questions embodied in the gestures of the old man: could the actor incarnate the whole world, nature itself? And could nature itself, with all its unpredictability, uniqueness, and constancy, reveal itself in the actor? Throughout his career, Grotowski showed little interest in actors who

Figure 1.2 Jerzy Grotowski in oasis Kara-kum (1956). Photographer unknown, courtesy of the Archive of the Grotowski Centre, Wroclaw

behave "naturally" on stage. Instead he sought those actors who reveal nature—their own personal nature as well as that of all humanity. Eventually, he would call this phenomenon **organicity**, one of the enduring searches of Grotowski's career.

THE POLITICAL GAME

When he returned to Poland in autumn 1956, Grotowski found the country embroiled in workers' riots. These protests, supported by many intellectuals and artists, came to be known as the Polish October and Grotowski, for the only time in his life, actively and publicly worked in a political forum. He became a leader of the youth movement calling for reforms and published several provocative articles. His activity stopped abruptly, however, in early 1957. It's possible the decision to halt his political activity was made under a certain amount of pressure, and even threats, from the authorities. Eighteen years later, when he spoke about this period of his life, he offered some insight: "I was so fascinated with **Gandhi** that I wanted to be like him. I found out that's impossible for objective reasons, and besides it would be against my nature, which is capable of fair play but cannot fully believe that everyone has good intentions" (cited in Osiński 1986: 20).

> **Mohandas Gandhi (1869–1948)**: India's spiritual and political leader who developed the practice of nonviolent civil disobedience in the country's struggle for independence.

As a theatre artist, Grotowski seemed to stay away from politics. In a country riddled by corruption and suffering under oppression, he steadfastly called his theatre work "apolitical." However, after his emigration from Poland in 1982, following the imposition of martial law in December 1981, Grotowski admitted, "I had to say I was not political in order to be political" (cited in Findlay 1986: 180). It's difficult now not to see the political overtones of *The Constant Prince* or *Apocalypsis cum figuris*. One could even go so far as to say that his work in and around theatre had major political repercussions for Poland. During the 1970s, Grotowski's paratheatre activities offered one example of freedom within the tyranny of the surrounding society. Many young Poles flocked to Grotowski's laboratory to taste something that was forbidden to them elsewhere. In his article "You are Someone's Son," composed in 1985, Grotowski speaks clearly of his politics:

> *I work, not to make some discourse, but to enlarge the island of freedom which I bear; my obligation is not to make political declarations, but to make holes in the wall.* The things which were forbidden before me should be permitted after me; the doors which were closed and double-locked should be opened.
> (Grotowski 1989: 294–5)

Is it possible to call such an attitude apolitical? Although his foray into active politics was brief, one of Grotowski's greatest legacies is precisely an example of a life lived toward freedom.

EARLY THEATRE WORK (1957–9)

After the Polish October, Grotowski worked in Krakow as an assistant professor in the Theatre School, directed productions for several repertory theatres, completed his master's project, won an award for his radio production of *Sakuntala* (based on the ancient dramatic poem by Kalidasa), and organized a series of public lectures on Asian themes. Grotowski also took two trips to France during these years and was strongly influenced by a meeting with mime master **Marcel Marceau (b. 1923)**.

Grotowski's early theatre work included productions of Eugene Ionesco's *The Chairs* and Anton Chekhov's *Uncle Vanya*. Both garnered mixed reviews from Polish critics. One can imagine the **existential** aesthetic of these early productions from the following description of Grotowski's master's project, Prosper Mérimée's *The Woman is a Devil*:

> The play was performed by a quartet of actors against a backdrop of black curtains. The costumes were limited to black sweaters and street clothes. A student...provided guitar accompaniment. The entire set consisted of four classroom desks and a colorful poster upstage saying "Kill Rats."
>
> (Osiński 1986: 24)

Existentialism: a movement in literature and philosophy that emphasizes the individual's isolation in a hostile world and taking responsibility for one's actions.

Grotowski directed two other productions during these Krakow years, both based on the same contemporary play, *The Ill-Fated Family*. The playwright described his play as a "good-natured, realistic comedy..." (cited in Osiński 1986: 24). Grotowski's two versions, on the other hand, were noted for their indebtedness to Meyerhold and Vakhtangov.

From his early theatre productions and writings, one can sense the burgeoning of Grotowski's ideas and ideals, his dissatisfaction with the state of theatre, and his commitment to artistic responsibility and ethics. During these years, he was shaping both the form of his future creative explorations and the objectives of his parallel agenda:

> I have chosen the artistic profession because I realized quite early that I am being haunted by a certain "thematic concern," a certain "leading motif," and a desire to reveal that "concern" and present it to other

people...I am haunted by the problem of human loneliness and the inevitability of death. But a human being (and here begins my "leading motif") is capable of acting against one's own loneliness and death. If one involves oneself in problems outside narrow spheres of interest,... if one recognizes the union of man and nature, if one is aware of the indivisible unity of nature and finds one's identity within it,...then one attains an essential degree of liberation.

(cited in Osiński 1986: 26–7)

In 1958, Grotowski plainly states his reasons for work in the theatre and clearly articulates his search for liberation. His quest, one of the most fascinating artistic journeys of the twentieth century, would last for more than 40 years through five distinct phases named by Grotowski himself: Theatre of Productions, Theatre of Participation (or Paratheatre), Theatre of Sources, Objective Drama, and Art as Vehicle (or Ritual Arts).

THEATRE OF PRODUCTIONS (1959–69)

A CHANCE MEETING

Ludwik Flaszen (b. 1930) was already a well-known literary and theatre critic when the city authorities from Opole, a small town in southern Poland, asked him to revitalize the tiny Theatre of 13 Rows. The theatre occupied a low-ceilinged room with a small proscenium stage and thirteen rows of seats. Flaszen felt incapable of assuming the role of director himself. He needed a collaborator more skilled in the practical aspects of theatre. One day while Flaszen was sitting in the journalist's club in Krakow contemplating his dilemma, Grotowski happened to walk by the window and Flaszen thought: "Why not?" (Barba 1999: 29). In May 1959, Flaszen invited Grotowski to join him in Opole. They hardly knew each other, but together they forged a plan for a new theatre.

THE THEATRE OF 13 ROWS

The conditions in Opole included the establishment of the post of Literary Director (to be filled by Flaszen), unlimited freedom in choice of the group and the repertoire, and adequate subsidy to work without interruption. Grotowski and Flaszen selected nine young actors to form the ensemble. Grotowski called them renegades and said that each one had a particular explosive quality. Among them were: Rena Mirecka (b. 1934), a graduate of the Krakow Theatre School, Zygmunt Molik (b. 1930), and Antoni Jahołkowski (1931–79). When Grotowski spoke of "renegades," he was referring as well to other actors who joined in later seasons: Zbigniew Cynkutis (1938–87), Ryszard Cieślak (1937–90), Stanisław Scierski (1939–83), Maja Komorowska (b. 1937), and South American actress Elizabeth Albahaca (b. 1937). These eight actors formed the core group that would be associated with Grotowski's work for the next 25 years.

The Theatre of 13 Rows began its first season in much the same manner as any repertory theatre operating in Poland at the time. The actors were given scripts for Jean Cocteau's *Orpheus* and told to have their lines memorized before the first rehearsal. Zygmunt Molik once commented that he was the only actor who arrived to that first rehearsal prepared. Rehearsals lasted three weeks. The length of the rehearsal periods, however, grew incrementally with each new production: the second production, six weeks of rehearsal; the third, three months; the fourth, six months; until the final theatre production, *Apocalypsis cum figuris*, which had 400 rehearsals over a three-year period.

Besides *Orpheus* (premiere October 8, 1959), in the first season, the troupe produced Byron's *Cain* (premiere January 30, 1960) and Mayakovsky's *Mystery Bouffe* (premiere July 31, 1960). Grotowski also directed Goethe's *Faust* (premiere April 13, 1960) at the Polski Theatre in Poznan. This was the only production he directed away from the Theatre of 13 Rows after founding the group. The second season in Opole consisted of Kalidasa's *Sakuntala* (premiere December 13, 1960), a brief montage of World War II images titled *The Tourists*, and Grotowski's first experiment with the **Polish Romantic** tradition, Adam Mickiewicz's classic text, *Forefather's Eve (Dziady)* (premiere June 6, 1961). During these first two seasons, the productions were not kept in repertory long. Program notes and random photographs give the only indication of the productions' qualities. But from these early sources, the major themes and contributions of Grotowski's research during Theatre of Productions can be discovered, including the concepts of **poor theatre**, **montage**, **the use of space**, and the **holy actor**.

POOR THEATRE

The term most commonly associated with Grotowski's work during Theatre of Productions is **poor theatre**. Poor Theatre can best be understood in relation to Rich Theatre. Rich and poor have little to do with economics, but refer instead to the number of other artistic disciplines and elements involved in a theatre production. When Ludwik Flaszen first coined the term "poor theatre," in writing about the company's production of *Akropolis* in 1962, he described a theatre where "it is absolutely forbidden to introduce into the play anything which is not already there at the very beginning" (Flaszen in Grotowski 2002: 75). Grotowski (Figure 1.3) took up poor theatre as a slogan and used it as the title of his seminal article "Towards a Poor Theatre" in 1965 (see Chapter 2). Grotowski asserts that theatre can exist without any accoutrements, needing only the live communion between actor and spectator, and he applies the term to all the practical work then taking place at the Theatre of 13 Rows. Grotowski's manifesto establishes poor theatre as an emblem for one of the twentieth century's most extensive theatre revolutions.

Figure 1.3 Jerzy Grotowski (1965). Photographer unknown, courtesy of the Archive of the Grotowski Centre, Wroclaw

First experiments

In the beginning of his work at the Theatre of 13 Rows, Grotowski experimented to discover a new theatrical form. The resulting productions looked strained and stilted. **Eugenio Barba**, who at the time was a scholarship student studying stage direction at the Theatre Academy in Warsaw, attended *Forefather's Eve (Dziady)* in 1961 and remarks how the performance struck him as "unpolished," dependent on university theatre conventions like direct contact with the audience, overacting, parody, and audience participation (Barba 1999: 20).

Eugenio Barba (b. 1936): Italian-born stage director and theorist. He founded Odin Teatret (Denmark) in 1964 and conducts research under his International School of Theatre Anthropology (ISTA).

In these early productions, Grotowski often imposed style and mannerisms on the actors. Later, he realized that directing a production is a process toward awareness and knowledge and not merely the chance to demonstrate things the director already knows. With each new production, Grotowski rigorously put aside the directorial concepts, scenic tricks, and other gimmicks that only served to clutter and confuse the scenic space, dramatic action, and, most importantly, the actor's personal process. He began to work systematically to build the actors' physical strength, stamina, and flexibility, while learning to pinpoint and nurture those aspects of the work that stemmed from his own creative consciousness and that of his actors. Step by step, Grotowski refined his concept of poor theatre, and the actor became more prominent in the director's lifelong search for liberation. However, there were several other areas of investigation simultaneously driving him in the same direction. The first of these is the treatment of the text.

TREATMENT OF TEXT (MONTAGE)

During the Theatre of Productions, all of Grotowski's performances, except his final one, *Apocalypsis cum figuris*, were based on established dramatic texts, especially those of the great **Polish Romantic** writers: Adam Mickiewicz (1798–1855), Juliusz Słowacki (1809–49), and Stanisław Wyspiański (1869–1907).

Polish Romanticism: emerged during the period between 1795 and the end of World War I (1919) when Poland was removed from the map of Europe, divided among Austria, Prussia, and Russia. While contemporaneous with French and German Romanticism, the Polish version owes little to their influence. The dramatic works of the Polish Romantic writers lyrically acclaim "the heroism of Polish patriots who, assuming the destiny of their oppressed people, rise to play witness to a subjected humanity which is promised happier days" (Temkine 1972: 67). These plays (e.g. *Dziady*, *Akropolis*, *Kordian*, *The Constant Prince*, *Samuel Zborowski*) remain regular features in the repertoire of Polish theatres even today.

Grotowski's relationship with these texts was not as an interpreter but more like an excavator, like someone digging for a secret. He freely adapted the texts of the Polish Romantics and reassembled them to convey a powerful message to his own time. He viewed the script in a very cinematic fashion and sometimes would insert texts from other sources into the play. He referred to this process as montage. However, his real innovation was to use the reworked text as a pretext for the actor's personal work. The playwright's words served as a runway for the actor to bring potent, personal images to life, authentically and with technical virtuosity. But before we discuss Grotowski's contributions to the art of the actor, let's examine his role in the transformation of the theatre space itself.

ACTOR/SPECTATOR/SPACE

In the first years of the Theatre of 13 Rows, Grotowski was obsessed with the relationship between actor, spectator, and space. Of course, other directors and theorists before him had proposed innovations in the theatre space or manipulated the actor–audience relationship, but Grotowski did not stop with the idea of a flexible performance space. Grotowski explored how space itself can become a part of the dramatic action and he strove to rid the theatre of illusory settings. He viewed each new production as a fresh experiment in the actor/audience spatial relationship and united all aspects of the production to create a living, dynamic space that functioned only for that particular work. Many of his ideas now define what we call **environmental theatre**.

Grotowski's theatre frees space from the limitations of design, concept, illusory effect, and convention. The space is what it is. The theatre as a safe, familiar place no longer exists and the participant (both actor and spectator) is forced into a new mode of awareness. American theatre critic Eric Bentley captures Grotowski's genius in his description of the three performances he viewed in New York in 1969:

> I very much admire the way in which each of your evenings was a separate exploration. I understand "environmental theatre" now, just as I now see what intimacy means. In *The Constant Prince*, we were medical students looking down on an operating table or a bullfight crowd looking down on the fight. In *Akropolis*, we were inside the world of the play and the players—within the electrified barbed wire of an extermination camp. In *Apocalypsis*, we were a small group of onlookers, small enough to feel ourselves disciples of the disciples... These events are planned as a whole: such and such actors to be seen by so and so many spectators from such and such an angle at such and such a distance.
>
> (Bentley 1969: 169–70)

Grotowski's companion in this actor–spectator–space exploration was often scenic architect **Jerzy Gurawski (b. 1935)**. Gurawski designed the space, objects, and costumes for *Dr. Faustus*, *Kordian*, and *The Constant Prince*, among others. In their work together, they explored the actor/spectator/space relationship using many of the devices that now permeate contemporary theatre. They changed the play's setting, placed audience members in direct contact with the actors, and even tried including spectators in the action of the play. But they soon gave up these ideas. Grotowski realized that coercing the audience to participate in the rehearsed actions of the performers only leads to more alienation, not authentic participation. Grotowsk~~i~~ special spectator.

> Personally, I am awaiting a spectator who would
> see the true aspect of his hidden nature. A spectator willing ⌐.
> into casting off the mask of life, a spectator ready to accept the attack, ⊔⊔⊔
> transgression of common norms and expectations, and who—thus denuded,
> thus disarmed, and moved by a sincerity bordering on the excessive—
> consents to contemplate his own personality.
>
> (cited in Kumiega 1985: 145–6)

Eventually, Grotowski realized that the fragmented aspects of contemporary society do not allow for actors and spectators to enter the theatre space with a common set of beliefs and, therefore, a psychophysical awakening and liberation on the part of the spectator cannot be guaranteed. The actor, however, might achieve the desired state of heightened sincerity. Thus, while the director could not determine the spectator's responses, the spectator could witness the actor's accomplishment and react to its reverberation: "If the actor, by setting himself a challenge publicly challenges others, and through excess, profanation, and outrageous sacrilege reveals himself by casting off his everyday mask, he makes it possible for the spectator to undertake a similar process of self-penetration" (Grotowski 2002: 34).

Finally, Grotowski did not propose any rules for the actor–spectator–space relationship. In fact, with *The Constant Prince* and *Apocalypsis*, he even returned to placing the spectators in a voyeuristic relationship to the production. What was essential in Grotowski's research was not the elimination of the stage or the mixing of the actors and spectators, but casting the spectator in a precise role in the production and determining the spectator's function in the space. Only then might the chasm between spectator and actor vanish.

Grotowski listened to the astute observations of companions like Barba, Flaszen, and Gurawski. He stimulated his actors to seek their own creative solutions to problems and rigorously critiqued them and himself. Slowly, Grotowski's vision of the theatre space and the actor's distinctive place in that space emerged.

LABORATORY THEATRE: THE SEARCH DEEPENS

In 1962, the Theatre of 13 Rows officially changed its name to the Laboratory Theatre of 13 Rows. This shift occurred just after the company's premiere of *Kordian* by Juliusz Slowacki on February 13, 1962. The new production and name change signaled the group's inclination toward disciplined research. Eugenio Barba arrived in Opole for a 30-month-long apprenticeship in January 1962. His impressions of *Kordian* differ radically from his review of *Dziady* several months earlier:

> I perceived a paradoxical logic which emphasized the text as though it were speaking of me and of the present. The way in which actors and spectators were distributed in the space was profoundly coherent. I was full of admiration for the dramatic solutions, the interpretation of the text and the actors' performance.
>
> (Barba 1999: 28)

In August 1962, Grotowski traveled to the People's Republic of China. In Shanghai, he met Dr Ling, a voice expert. They discussed respiration techniques and the use of the various vocal resonators, and Dr Ling taught Grotowski how to check if an actor's larynx is open or closed during voice production. Grotowski made other discoveries in China. For example, he observed how the actors of the Peking Opera begin each action with a distinct movement in the opposite direction from where they want to go. He used this tool with his actors in Poland, where it came to be called "the Chinese principle" (Barba 1999: 53).

Upon his return to Opole, Grotowski continued rehearsals of Stanislaw Wyspianski's *Akropolis* (see Chapter 3), which had begun in March 1962. The first version of this performance opened on October 10, 1962 and was immediately recognized as a landmark production. *Akropolis* remained in the company's repertory for almost eight years in five different versions.

After *Akropolis*, the company began work on Christopher Marlowe's *The Tragical History of Doctor Faustus*, which premiered April 23, 1963. During the work on *Dr. Faustus*, the company's daily training and research into vocal and physical exercises intensified. While rehearsing *Akropolis*, exercises were undertaken to resolve particular technical and aesthetic problems the actors encountered in their struggle to embody the reality of a concentration camp in an unsentimental manner. After *Akropolis* premiered, the actors continued to meet daily for training. They eliminated those exercises directly linked to the needs of a specific performance and selected psychophysical exercises that had creative value on their own. Grotowski now established a way of working with the actors that he would use throughout his career. He assigned each actor to become expert in a particular kind of exercise. As the actor struggled to master the exercises and teach them to the others, Grotowski served as observer and critic. In time, the exercises of the Laboratory Theatre began to function on two levels: as basic work on elements of craft and as spiritual work on oneself. Grotowski carefully hid this aspect of his work, even though Stanislavsky had used similar terminology, because such a "mystical" attitude did not curry favor with the government authorities and the Laboratory's Theatre continued existence was precarious.

Seeking allies

Grotowski always believed in the importance of allies. He was expert at meeting people on their own terms and convincing them to support his mission. Whether it be singing Polish Christmas carols all night with a censor in Opole, sharing a bottle of vodka with an immigration officer while being held in a Miami airport, or waxing poetic to Soviet agents on the importance of "beauty" in the theatre—Grotowski did what he needed to do to keep the authorities at bay and continue the ever-increasing momentum of the performance work and research. Once he put the whole company on vacation in the middle of winter in an effort to outfox the authorities that were threatening to close the theatre. In Poland, at that time, nobody could get fired while on vacation. He patiently sat through endless bureaucratic meetings and had the company keep a weekly log of their communist party meetings. It was entirely fabricated. He once revealed, "I have often lied, but I have never compromised." He built many alliances, friends, and supporters, both in and out of Poland, but the general public, the theatre establishment, and many critics failed to recognize the relevance of Grotowski's research theatre.

During the Tenth Congress of the International Theatre Institute (ITI) held in Warsaw in June 1963, Eugenio Barba "borrowed" a state-owned bus and transported approximately thirty of the most prestigious conference participants to the city of Lodz where they attended a performance of *Dr. Faustus*, barred from the "official" program of the conference as planned by the Polish authorities. The next morning there was a huge commotion on the convention floor as those who had seen the performance lauded Grotowski and his collaborators. They returned to their home countries and wrote fervent articles about Grotowski's laboratory. Barba's escapade garnered the company unprecedented international attention.

During work on the next production, *The Hamlet Study*, based on Stanisław Wyspiański's version of Shakespeare's play, the crisis with the authorities reached its peak. The company's subsidies were cut and everyone worked without assurance of being paid. There was no money available to even print programs or take photographs for *The Hamlet Study*, which premiered in March 1964. Presented as an "open rehearsal," there were only about twenty performances, and it is often cited as Grotowski's one "failure." However, he contended that the process of collective creation explored during rehearsals for *The Hamlet Study* was fundamental in determining the future path of the group and led directly to the way of developing *Apocalypsis cum figuris* some years later.

In summer 1964, an event occurred that forged the company's future. The two directors of the Laboratory Theatre of 13 Rows accepted an invitation to relocate their activities to the city of Wroclaw, a large industrial and university town in southwestern Poland. On January 1, 1965, the Laboratory Theatre officially moved to a three-story building in Wroclaw's central marketplace. Everything was now in place for Grotowski and his company to meet the world.

THE HOLY ACTOR

Grotowski aimed to "rediscover" the elements of the theatre by eliminating everything superfluous and focus on the very essence of the art form: the actor. He makes the distinction between the "courtesan actor" (who exploits his body for money and fame) and the "holy actor" (who undertakes a process of **self-penetration**, sacrificing his body, not selling it). The courtesan actor works through the accumulation of skills and effects; the holy actor's process of self-penetration involves a *via negativa*, a "technique of elimination," ridding the organism of its resistance to the psychophysical process of playing a role. For one, the body becomes dense—for the other, the body becomes transparent.

With his next production, *The Constant Prince*, Grotowski, together with actor Ryszard Cieślak, accomplished this aim. The actor's performance became a vehicle for self-study and self-exploration, a field for work on one's self and individual transcendence. Most descriptions of Cieślak's performance in *The Constant Prince* communicate with amazement and deep respect his radiance, agility, simplicity, technical mastery, and complete commitment to each moment of the psychophysical score. This is how the role penetrates the actor: through continuous work on the technical elements until all physical and psychological obstacles dissolve. Sacrifice occurs when the actor reveals something precious and personal as a gift to the audience through detailed work on structure and self.

Ryszard Cieślak exemplified the **holy actor**. He let fall the mask of daily life, penetrated his own experience, and stripped himself bare— Grotowski called this **"the total act"**:

> At the moment when the actor attains this, he becomes a phenomenon *hic et nunc*; this is neither a story nor the creation of an illusion; it is the present moment. The actor exposes himself and . . . he discovers himself. Yet he has to know how to do this anew each time . . . This human phenomenon, the actor, whom you have before you, has transcended the state of his division or duality. This is no longer acting, and this is why it is an act (actually what you want to do every day of your life is to act). This is the phenomenon of total action. That is why one wants to call it a total act.
>
> (cited in Osiński 1986: 86)

After *The Constant Prince* premiered in Wroclaw in April 1965, Grotowski focused even more on *via negativa* and poor theatre—those principles which guided Cieślak's liberated and luminous performance. As the company commenced an extended period of travel and international acclaim, inside the Laboratory Theatre's walls, in the privacy of their studio, Grotowski was determined to create the conditions for each actor to accomplish the total act.

GROTOWSKI MEETS THE WORLD

At the Second World Festival of Student Theatres in Nancy, France (1965), Grotowski led seminars and, along with Ryszard Cieślak and Rena Mirecka, conducted demonstrations of the Laboratory Theatre's physical and vocal exercises. Similar seminars were held in Paris, Padua, Milan, Rome, and London. Also in 1965, Eugenio Barba's book, *In Search of the Lost Theatre*, was published in Italian and the American theatre journal, *Tulane Drama Review*, edited by **Richard Schechner**, dedicated a large part of one issue to the Laboratory Theatre's achievements.

Richard Schechner (b. 1933): director of the Performance Group and a major figure in the founding of the Performance Studies program at New York University. As editor of *Tulane Drama Review* (now *The Drama Review*) he was one of the leading exponents of Grotowski's work in the English-speaking world.

In February 1966, the Laboratory Theatre began its first foreign tour. *The Constant Prince* was performed in Sweden, Denmark, and Norway. The second foreign tour took place in the summer when performances of *The Constant Prince* in Paris and Amsterdam caused a great sensation. In August 1966, **Peter Brook** invited Grotowski to conduct a course for the Royal Shakespeare Company in London. According to Brook, this encounter provoked a massive creative shock in the British-trained actors (Brook 1968b: 11).

Peter Brook (b. 1925): theatre director (Figure 1.4). In 1970, he founded the International Centre for Theatre Research in Paris. His productions, including *A Midsummer Night's Dream*, *Marat/Sade*, *Conference of the Birds*, and *The Mahabarata*, have been acclaimed around the world. He remained always a profound friend and supporter of Grotowski's work.

Prior to the official opening of their next production in 1969, the Laboratory Theatre performed *The Constant Prince* and/or *Akropolis* throughout Europe and in Mexico. Workshops, seminars, and conferences were often presented in association with these performances. In November 1967, Grotowski and Cieślak conducted a four-week seminar for advanced acting students at New York University.

Figure 1.4 Jerzy Grotowski and Peter Brook (1975). Photographer unknown, courtesy of the Archive of the Grotowski Centre, Wroclaw

During these years of travel and international acclaim, Grotowski had several important meetings. He first met American director **Joseph Chaikin (1935–2003)** in London in 1966. Chaikin and his **Open Theatre** claimed to be influenced greatly by Grotowski's work. Grotowski admired the group's discipline, integrity, and personal response to the Laboratory Theatre's methodology. "they [the Open Theatre] do not ape us in anything. They seek their own way and at their own risk. Only this form of reference to our experiences with method can have any meaning whatsoever" (cited in Osiński 1986: 109).

Grotowski and Artaud

Comparisons are often drawn between Grotowski and French actor, poet, director, and theatre theorist **Antonin Artaud (1896–1948)**. Artaud's "theatre of cruelty" ideas, conceived to provoke the audience's complacency, had gained much popularity in avant-garde theatre circles in the 1960s. However, Grotowski always claimed that he didn't read about Artaud until very late in his own explorations and he preferred to place himself in Stanislavsky's line of technique and thought.

Notwithstanding, in 1967, upon publication of the Polish edition of Artaud's book, *The Theatre and Its Double*, Grotowski wrote a beautiful homage to Artaud. In the article, "He Wasn't Entirely Himself," Grotowski challenges Artaud's contributions as a theatre practitioner, but recognizes his importance as a visionary and a "poet of the possibilities of the theatre" (Grotowski 2002: 125).

ANOTHER NAME CHANGE

In September 1966, the Laboratory Theatre of 13 Rows formally changed its name to the Laboratory Theatre Research Institute of Acting Method, marking the group's interest in pursuing their research aims and the dissemination of their findings concerning actor-training techniques. While in residence in Wroclaw, the actors performed, trained, worked with a growing number of foreign students, and prepared their new production. The new production was based on Słowacki's *Samuel Zborowski*. Rehearsals, which began in December 1965, extended over a three-year period. During that time, the premiere was postponed several times and the title of the piece changed to *The Gospels* and then finally to *Apocalypsis cum figuris*. After an open rehearsal on July 19, 1968, the performance officially premiered on February 11, 1969.

A CRISIS OF CREATION

1968—the world is in chaos. In Prague, Baghdad, Montreal, Lima, Paris, and Chicago, students and the oppressed rebel, wars escalate, regimes fall, and leaders are assassinated. In Poland, the government initiates a campaign of anti-Semitism, following the 1967 Arab–Israeli war, which results in "ousting over nine thousand people from positions of authority, all of them either Jews or revisionists" (Halecki cited in Cioffi 1996: 96). Persecution of Jews in Poland attains an intensity not seen since the Nazi occupation. The climax occurs in August when Poland joins in the Soviet invasion of Czechoslovakia to quash the political reforms and liberalization that came to be called the Prague Spring.

The turmoil around the world, especially Poland's descent into its anti-Semitic habits, touched Grotowski in a deeply personal way. He even appealed to Eugenio Barba to send him some poison because he feared arrest and imprisonment and wanted a means to retain his dignity if danger threatened (Barba 1999: fn. 171). The events of 1968 corresponded to a time of intense change in Grotowski's creative process and his chosen path.

Apocalypsis cum figuris, Grotowski's masterpiece and final theatre production, had a difficult birth. At one point, the group had over 20 hours of material. The actors became nervous and overacted. They were repeating what they already knew how to do. Grotowski reduced the number of actors. He changed the source material from *Samuel Zborowski* to *The Gospels*. Still the performance remained unborn. Finally, in one rehearsal a mistake was made: Anton Jahołkowski, in his role as Simon Peter, chose Zbigniew Cynkutis to be the Christ figure instead of Ryszard Cieślak. Suddenly, the dynamics of the process crystallized. Something unspoken had been made flesh. The solution was not to illustrate the myth, but to bring it into reality, here and now.

Grotowski began to ask the actors for a more personal response to the material of the Gospels. Each actor confronted a series of essential questions: "What would have happened to Christ if he revealed himself nowadays? In a literal way. What would we do with him? How would we see him? Where would he reveal himself? Would he be noticed at all?" (Flaszen cited in Kumiega 1985: 91). Rena Mirecka recalls being told, time after time, "I don't believe what you're doing." She returned to her room to dig deeper, to reveal more. More than 30 years later, tears still came to her eyes as she remembered the difficulty of this process.

Grotowski tried different tactics to bring forth the life of the new performance. For almost one year, he gave no notes to the actors. Finally, he decided to leave the rehearsal hall and let the actors work without the pressure of his presence. After one month, he came back to the theatre and saw that the actors, while still nervous, now "dared to do" and what he saw them doing showed signs of life.

Then the problem of "the true and only the true" appeared. Grotowski admits that in previous performances there had been elements that were not true, where the truth had remained hidden behind the structure. This time Grotowski refused to pretend. He wanted each actor to reveal his/her mystery. And he, as director, approached his own mystery. As he whispered to the actors, "Do!," he drew closer to his own nature. *Apocalypsis*, Grotowski's final theatre production, was also his most personal.

When rehearsals entered their final phase, the company felt itself on the threshold of a new possibility. Each transmutation of *Apocalypsis* was like an old skin falling off, revealing a performance farther and farther from theatre and nearer and nearer to something other—still unnamed.

APOCALYPSIS CUM FIGURIS

Apocalypsis cum figuris (the title stems from **Thomas Mann**'s novel, *Doctor Faustus*) demonstrated Grotowski's principles of poor theatre, total act, and the possibilities of the actor–spectator relationship and extended them in a whole new direction. In an empty room, only the spectators and the actors defined the space. Stage objects were reduced to a loaf of bread, a knife, a white cloth, candles, and a bucket of water. Two spotlights, positioned on the floor and focused toward the walls, achieved all the lighting effects. At one moment, the room was plunged into darkness and only candles, precisely positioned, lit the actors' radiant bodies. The actual text was selected and put together only during the final stages of rehearsal. The dialogue was drawn from the Bible, Dostoevsky's *The Brothers Karamazov*, **T.S. Eliot**, and **Simone Weil**. Witnesses of *Apocalypsis* speak of the quality of the vocal work in the production—its power, precision, and musicality.

Thomas Mann (1875–1955): German writer whose work often dealt with the artist's role in society. He won the Nobel Prize for Literature in 1929. His most famous works include *The Magic Mountain* (1924) and *Death in Venice* (1912).

T.S. Eliot (1888–1965): American-born poet who lived in England for most of his life. His poem "The Wasteland" is considered one of the masterpieces of the twentieth century. He won the Nobel Prize for Literature in 1948.

Simone Weil (1909–43): French philosopher and mystic. She viewed suffering as a bridge to God. Her works include *The Need for Roots* (1952) and *Waiting for God* (1951), both published posthumously.

After its official premiere in 1969, *Apocalypsis* toured the world and fueled the reputation of Grotowski and his actors. What made this production so important? *Apocalypsis* can be viewed as a contemporary passion play. In a brutal and blasphemous manner, Grotowski's actors incarnate the Christ myth before the spectator's eyes. However, Grotowski made no attempt at universal meaning or catharsis which might result in the conventional reactions of empathy or emotional release in the spectator:

> His aim, therefore, is to bring us momentarily into contact with the deepest levels within ourselves, deeper than those engaged within the order of forms, through incarnate mythic confrontation. If we succeed, through the shock of exposure, in touching those depths, we are changed forever. The process does not involve release; it is rather a re-awakening, or a re-birth, and in consequence potentially painful.
>
> (Kumiega 1985: 97)

Grotowski never stopped believing in the possibility of change, both within the actor and the spectator. If he rejected the concept of catharsis it was because he believed that such an overtly emotional response actually prevents real change from occurring. Eric Bentley's reaction to *Apocalypsis* reveals the true power of what was happening in the space between the actors and the spectators during the performance and why, as a theatre event, it remains a profound accomplishment:

> During the show *Apocalypsis*, something happened to me. I put it this personally because it was something very personal that happened. About halfway through the play I had a quite specific illumination. A message came to me—from nowhere, as they say—about my private life and self. This message must stay private, to be true to itself, but the fact that it arrived has public relevance, I think, and I should publicly add that I don't recall this sort of thing happening to me in the theatre before . . .
>
> (Bentley 1969: 167)

Apocalypsis cum figuris was performed until 1980, undergoing several major transformations. The actors' symbolic white costumes eventually were replaced with their own clothes. The benches were removed and spectators sat or stood around the periphery of the space. At one point in the work on the production, spectators were even invited to participate in the action. This was a very brief experiment. However, the real innovation in *Apocalypsis* was the aspect of not-pretending. The themes of personal honesty and renunciation were made palpable in the theatre space and a new relationship between actor and spectator, one based on sincerity, not illusion or pretence, was able to occur. When *Apocalypsis* finally was born, it formed a perfect bridge into the next frontier of Grotowski's research: The Theatre of Participation or Paratheatre.

THE PEAK OF SUCCESS

From 1968–70, Grotowski traveled extensively. He made four solitary trips to India: at the end of 1968, in the summer of 1969, at the end of 1969, and in the summer of 1970. From late August through late November 1968, the company toured to the Edinburgh International Festival, the Cultural Olympics at the Olympic Summer Games in Mexico City, and to France. It was also during this tour that *Akropolis* was filmed in London. Peter Brook provided an introduction and Grotowski himself oversaw the final editing. Shown on American television on Sunday evening, January 12, 1969, the film was "received coolly" (Anthony G. Bowman cited in Osinski 1986: 116).

Grotowski was invited to Belgrade as honorary guest of the International Festival of Research Theatres in September 1969. While there, he cemented his reputation for severity. Grotowski leveled harsh criticism at the performances he saw, including some of the world's most significant experimental companies, and dismissed the vapid imitations of the Laboratory Theatre's training methods. "These were four hours of unending public confessions and analyses of world theatre. The Polish director settled accounts with the entire avant-garde . . . " (Franco Quadri cited in Osinski 1986: 117). He then traveled with the troupe to the United States with three productions: *Akropolis*, *The Constant Prince*, and *Apocalypsis cum figuris*.

GROTOWSKI MEETS THE UNITED STATES

The Laboratory Theatre had planned to visit the United States the previous year, but the group was denied entry after the Soviet Union invaded Czechoslovakia. A petition protesting the State Department's decision signed by sixty high-profile representatives of the American theatre, including Arthur Miller, Edward Albee, Ellen Stewart, and

Jerome Robbins, was published in the *New York Times* on September 18, 1968. Eventually, permission was granted for a five-week stay in New York. This stay ended up lasting more than two months, from October 12 to December 17, 1969. Forty-eight performances of the three productions were given at the Washington Square Methodist Church in Greenwich Village, and four public meetings were held with Grotowski at the Brooklyn Academy of Music.

In New York, Grotowski and the Laboratory Theatre attained the pinnacle of their success. Tickets to the performances, each with a strictly limited number of seats, were hard to come by. Grotowski was ruthless with the lackadaisical American audience: no latecomers, no standing room, no exceptions! Despite the hoopla, the majority of American critics saluted the Polish Laboratory Theatre's presence as the most important theatre event of the year, and *Time* magazine selected the performances as the most important of the decade. Ryszard Cieślak was awarded two 1969 Obie (Off-Broadway Theatre) awards for his work in *The Constant Prince*: Best Actor and Most Promising Newcomer. He was the first actor to win both awards simultaneously and the first winner to act in a language other than English. *Apocalypsis* won the Drama Desk award for Best Production 1969–70.

Grotowski's arrival in the United States had been well prepared. *The Drama Review* had devoted several issues to analyzing the Polish company's work. Peter Brook's book, *The Empty Space*, published in 1968, contained a chapter entitled, "The Holy Theatre," in which he paid homage to Grotowski's endeavors. At the same time, Grotowski's own book, *Towards a Poor Theatre*, appeared in print. Published in English under the editorship of Eugenio Barba, the book gathered together several of Grotowski's major pronouncements, interviews, articles by Flaszen and Barba, descriptions of the company's exercises, and notes on workshops and classes. The book was translated into numerous languages and rapidly became a manual for experimental groups around the world.

Grotowski's various travels and meetings, the world's disorder, and his personal crises were manifestly leading him to a drastic decision. In late February 1970, he met with the editors of various Polish publications. At this point, when the Laboratory Theatre and Grotowski himself were at the top of their success, he said:

> We live in a post-theatrical epoch. What follows is not a new wave of theatre but rather something that will replace it... I feel that *Apocalypsis cum figuris*

is a new stage for me in my research. We have crossed a certain barrier.

(cited in Osiński 1986: 120)

But what lay on the other side of the barrier?

THEATRE OF PARTICIPATION/ PARATHEATRE (1969–78)

AWAY FROM THEATRE

Grotowski was at a crossroads—personally and professionally. He began to ask himself: "What does one do in such a case? One can force oneself to continue, but one must have a very strong character, because there is something wretched in that; . . . you can seek refuge in illness . . . or become a professor or rector and create some sort of extraspecial theatre school, which I thought about for awhile . . . " (cited in Osinski 1986: 122). Grotowski often advised others to travel when they faced major life questions and so, taking his own advice, he began a period of wandering: "It was, quite literally, a ramble through the continents involving direct meetings with people and places. Also, in a different sense, it was a journey away from the theatre to the roots of culture, to essential communication and perception" (Kolankiewicz 1978: 1).

Who did Grotowski meet and what did he do "on the road?" There is some speculation that Grotowski met **Carlos Castaneda (1925–98)**, an anthropologist who wrote about a Yacqui shaman named Don Juan. His writings detail an apprentice's initiation into a traditional and mystical field of knowledge. Grotowski certainly read these books and even referred to them often, but he maintained that he never met Castaneda. He did, however, visit the Esalen Institute, a center of the "human potential movement" in California. He hitchhiked incognito across North America, read **Jack Kerouac**, and listened to Bob Dylan. He even ventured cautiously into the realm of the New Age and the books of scientist **John C. Lilly**. Later, in the early 1980s, he encountered the work of Jungian **Arnold Mindell**. What Schechner refers to as "The American Connection," however, never exerted as much influence on Grotowski as India.

> **Jack Kerouac (1922–69)**: American writer of the Beat Generation. His books are often autobiographical and include *On the Road* (1957) and *The Dharma Bums* (1958).

> **John C. Lilly (1915–2001)**: an important member of the California counterculture group of scientists, mystics, and scholars of the 1960s and 1970s. His research into the nature of consciousness involved such tools as the isolation tank, dolphin communication, and hallucinogenic drugs.

> **Arnold Mindell (b. 1940)**: American psychotherapist who founded process-oriented psychology. His books include *Dreambody: The Body's Role in Revealing the Self* (1982).

In India, Grotowski traveled to the shrine of **Ramakrishna**, the Himalayas, and Bodh Gaya, where the Buddha received enlightenment. He met spiritual teachers, like the famed **Mother of Pondicherry**, and a **Baul** master with whom he exchanged ideas about the objective elements of the anatomy of the actor (Barba 1999: 169). Grotowski found his bearings in India. After six weeks in India and Kurdistan in 1970, Grotowski reencountered his Polish colleagues at the airport in Shiraz, Iran, and nobody recognized him. He had grown a beard and lost more than 80 pounds. While the company performed throughout Iran and Lebanon, Grotowski flew to Colombia where the anxious group of Latin American theatre artists awaited his arrival on the tarmac in Manizales.

> **Ramakrishna (1836–86)**: Hindu mystic who believed that all religions are pathways to approach freedom.

Mother of Pondicherry (1878–1973): Paris-born Mirra Alfassa, assisted spiritual teacher **Sri Aurobindo (1872–1950)** and supervised their ashram in Pondicherry, India.

THE TRANSFORMATION

The culmination of Grotowski's transformation took place in Colombia. There he speaks for the first time of theatre in the past tense and articulates the new direction his work will take: "This is a dual moment in my life. That which is theatre, 'technique', and methodology is behind me. That which has been reaching for other horizons within me has finally resolved itself..." (cited in Osiński 1986: 123). He discloses in a personal tone what was essential in his experience with theatre—the technique, the professionalism, the vocation itself. But the end result is that the vocation "has led me out of the theatre, out of technique, and out of professionalism." In Colombia, Grotowski redefines theatre as "a group and a place." He continues: "And, yes, it [theatre] can be indispensable to life, if one seeks a space where one does not lie to oneself. Where we do not conceal where we are, what we are, and where that which we do is what it is and we do not pretend it is anything else... And this, in time, will lead us out of the theatre..." (cited in Osiński 1986: 123). After moving "Towards a Poor Theatre," Grotowski was now moving away from theatre entirely.

THE DAY THAT IS HOLY

At the same time Grotowski was in Colombia articulating his new direction, a public call went out to young people in Poland to come to Wrocław to work, not on theatre but beyond it. Grotowski had composed this request, entitled "A Proposal for Working Together," in June, prior to leaving Poland for his six weeks in India and Kurdistan. This sequence of events demonstrates that Grotowski's transformation was not the direct result of some sudden illumination during his sojourn in India. In fact, Grotowski first spoke of the need to enlarge the company in February 1970. He was seeking young people who could assimilate themselves into the workings of the Laboratory Theatre easily. More than 300 responded.

Grotowski constructed the paradigm for this new period of work during a series of meetings in New York in December 1970. It had been one year since the Laboratory Theatre's triumphant New York tour, and hundreds of curious actors, directors, students, and professors crowded into Town Hall to hear Grotowski talk about theatre and question him about his group's controversial methods. Instead, the bearded wanderer stunned the group, talking seriously and openly, until four o'clock in the morning, about his concept of "Holiday." The Americans wanted to talk about practical things: nudity on stage, responsibility to the audience, methodology, and talent. Grotowski tolerantly answered their queries, always framing his answers in his new language. Armed with the foundation of craft and with his ever-present "hidden agenda" guiding him, Grotowski commenced the second major period of his research: Theatre of Participation or Paratheatre (1969–78).

In Poland, Grotowski wanted a complete change of atmosphere. The Laboratory Theatre acquired an abandoned farm about 40 kilometers from Wroclaw. After some structural reparations, the group's new activities were moved to this isolated, rural setting called Brzezinka, the name of the village nearby. Prior to moving, however, Grotowski began to work with a group of ten people in the Wroclaw space in order to establish a common meeting ground with the older members of the company. The original group of ten was soon reduced to four who were joined by three new arrivals. The selection period and initial preparation ended in November 1972, when a group of fourteen went to work in Brzezinka for three weeks. Seven of this group were new members and included **Włodzimierz Staniewski**. The other seven were old members of the Laboratory Theatre, including Grotowski himself.

> **Włodzimierz Staniewski (b. 1950)**: founder and director of the Center for Theatre Practices "Gardzienice" in a village in eastern Poland, one of the most important experimental companies working in the world today.

WHAT IS PARATHEATRE?

Paratheatre means, literally, alongside theatre, on the borders of theatre, or expanding its limits. It is sometimes paired with Active Culture. Active Culture, Grotowski says, is commonly called creativity. It is action "which gives a sense of fulfillment of life, an extending of its dimensions, is needed by many, and yet remains the domain of very few" (cited in Kumiega 1985: 201). To put it simply: Paratheatre/Active Culture seeks to extend the privilege of creative action to those not usually involved in theatre production.

In a series of lectures at the University of Rome more than a decade later, Grotowski remarked that his initial interest in paratheatre began at the end of the 1960s when a different kind of spectator appeared at the performances of the Laboratory Theatre—a more active spectator, more alive and engaged in the performance. From this point, the performances began to function as a "situation which gave us the possibility to meet other people who shared our nostalgia or our needs (or what we considered our needs)" (Grotowski 1982: 156). The problem then arose how to involve this new spectator-friend directly in the process of sacrifice and stripping away long practiced by the actors of the Laboratory Theatre; to involve the spectator-friend, not as a witness, but in an equal and reciprocal manner.

Little is known about the period of closed work from 1970–3. Grotowski states that "In the first years, when a small group worked thoroughly for months and months, and was later joined only by a few new participants from the outside, things happened which were on the border of a miracle" (Grotowski 1995: 120). There were never observers in the paratheatre work, only participants. Grotowski and his young group tackled the problem of how to involve these participants directly in the creative process; how to release in each one a flow of energy and arrive to a more authentic spontaneity. In order to accomplish this, there had to be a period of **disarmament**—a confrontation with one's social masks, personal clichés, and a ridding of fear and distrust to reveal a state of vulnerability. This period was followed by a release of simple, human expression—**the meeting**. It can be said that this process of disarmament and meeting was ever-present in the Laboratory Theatre's work. However, now theatre itself was eliminated.

The upkeep and renovation of Brzezinka and its surrounding fields and forests created a rhythm of work different from the more harsh life in the city. The alternation between work in the country, work in the city, and periods of time free spent with family and friends offered the possibility to develop a new relationship to nature (not to be understood as a return to nature or a romanticization of nature), which would become an integral aspect of Grotowski's continuing research.

The company's old hierarchy disintegrated and the new members often led the paratheatre activities.

The closed work continued in Wroclaw and Brzezinka until June 1973, when the first paratheatre meeting was organized with selected guests. It lasted for three days and three nights. The event, initially called *Holiday*, was eventually referred to as *Special Project*. It was during this period that **Jacek Zmysłowski (1953–82)**, who participated in these first public sessions and would become an important leader in the later phases of the research, was added to the paratheatre team.

PARATHEATRE ABROAD

During summer 1973, Grotowski traveled to the United States, New Zealand, Canada, Australia, and Japan. He gave lectures and planned the company's first major paratheatre tour. In Japan, he met **Tadashi Suzuki**. They attended a Nô Theatre rehearsal and visited Tokyo by night.

Tadashi Suzuki (b. 1939): Japanese director who developed the Suzuki Method of Actor Training, a strenuous, physical approach.

In September–October 1973, the Laboratory Theatre presented fourteen performances of *Apocalypsis* in Philadelphia and theatre workshops at the University of Pittsburgh. The group then retreated to a rural campground near Pittsburgh to conduct a *Special Project* which lasted eight days. The company repeated this format (with some variations) in France in November 1973 and in Australia from late March through mid-June 1974. In Australia, the paratheatre events were divided in two different projects: *Narrow Special Project* (devoted to the individual work of participants and of particular interest to Grotowski) and *Large Special Project* (focused more on group work).

During the 1974/75 season, the company stayed in Wroclaw and opened the paratheatre work to an increasing number of participants. Members of the Laboratory Theatre led a variety of workshops, for example, *Acting Therapy*, which focused on the Laboratory Theatre's vocal work and the elimination of psychophysical blocks; *Meditations Aloud*, conducted by Flaszen, which were more theoretical and intended to liberate the participants' ability to listen; *International Studio*, primarily involving non-Poles; and *Special Project*, where "The aim was Meeting, conceived of as an inter-human encounter, where man would be himself, regain the unity of his being, become creative and spontaneous in relation to others" (cited in Kumiega 1985: 176).

THE UNIVERSITY OF RESEARCH (1975)

In June–July 1975, the University of Research of the Theatre of Nations was held in Wroclaw, under the sponsorship of the Laboratory Theatre. Over 4,500 people participated in a variety of classes, seminars, workshops, performances, public meetings, films, demonstrations, and paratheatre events. A host of theatre royalty attended, including Peter Brook, Joseph Chaikin, Eugenio Barba, **Jean-Louis Barrault**, **Luca Ronconi**, and **André Gregory**. The premise was "to seek a basic ground of understanding between people . . . a new form of encounter with mankind," and for theatre professionals "to seek a new vital base for practicing one's profession" (cited in Osiński 1986: 151).

Jean-Louis Barrault (1910–94): French actor and director who worked with Antonin Artaud and trained under mime master Etienne Decroux (1898–1991). Famous for his role in the film *Children of Paradise* (1945).

Luca Ronconi (b. 1933): Italian stage director whose production *Orlando Furioso* (1969) brought him to international fame.

André Gregory (b. 1934): American actor and director (Figure 1.5). He founded The Manhattan Project and has appeared in numerous films, most famously *My Dinner with André* (1981), which discusses his work in Poland. André and his wife Mercedes (Chiquita) (1936–92) were two of Grotowski's closest friends and supporters.

Figure 1.5 Jerzy Grotowski and André Gregory (1975). Photograph by Joanna Drankowska

Paratheatre events organized for the University of Research took two basic forms: General Laboratory, open to anyone willing to participate, and including daily workshops as well as a nightly worksession called *Ul* (*Beehive*) (see Chapter 3); and specialized workshops, requiring a direct invitation from Grotowski, organized by individual members of the paratheatre team. The specialized workshops lasted up to 48 hours and took place in various locations—Brzezinka, the countryside around Wroclaw, or in the Laboratory Theatre building.

The University of Research was an ambitious and pioneering event, but its significance has never been assessed. For three weeks, Grotowski's laboratory became the Mecca of the theatre world and the nature and meaning of the art form was analyzed, questioned, and dreamed. Peter Brook discussed his company's trip to Africa and Eugenio Barba shed light on Odin Teatret's stay in southern Italy. Both of these directors had begun a period of experimentation in intercultural exchange, stimulated by Grotowski's research, which would reverberate across world theatre for the next 25 years. Gregory and Chaikin lamented the state of American experimental theatre and relished the optimism and boldness of the Polish meeting. Gregory stated, "It seems to me that this is a kind of revolution—not political, but creative. A kind of revolution because it says 'yes' to life and 'no' to death" (cited in Kolankeiwicz 1978: 45).

After the University of Research, the Laboratory Theatre took its program to the Venice Biennale. In Italy, Grotowski engaged in several analysis sessions of the paratheatre activities, while the debate about this new phase of his work burned up the Polish press. At home, Grotowski was accused of guruism, mystic murkiness, and succumbing to what is fashionable. He seldom responded to such attacks. His response was in the work itself and the reactions of the numerous participants.

TOWARD THE MOUNTAIN

In 1976, the Laboratory Theatre instituted *Otwarcia* (*Openings*) in Wroclaw. These experimental workshops were structured in a similar manner to *Beehives* and were open to anyone capable of active participation. From the beginning of May to the end of July, the company moved its projects to an historic monastery and rundown chateau near Saintes in southwestern France. This was the first time the Laboratory Theatre toured abroad without a theatre production. After Grotowski announced the project in an interview in the French newspaper, *Le Monde*, over 2,000 applications came in from around the world. Grotowski selected approximately 200 persons to participate in workshops and paratheatre events. **Jairo Cuesta (b. 1951)** was among those selected by Grotowski to begin work with him on a new, unnamed project.

In autumn 1976, plans were in full swing for *The Mountain Project*, the next major paratheatre event. Jacek Zmysłowski had accomplished a breakthrough with a small international group of non-professional young people in France:

> We led highly intensive open-air work which lasted several days and con-
> sisted—to put it simply—of movement, of the perception of space through
> movement, being in space in continual movement... It became possible to
> eliminate everything artificial and leave the most simple of relationships:
> an individual/space...
>
> (cited in Kumiega 1985: 193)

Grotowski, who had envisioned a mountain-themed project even before the University of Research, placed the entire project under Zmysłowski's direction. *The Mountain Project* was organized in three parts: *Nocne Czuwanie (Night Vigils)*, *Droga (The Way)*, and *Góra Płomienia (Mountain of Flame)*. Following *The Mountain Project*, Jacek Zmysłowski organized an event simply called *Czuwania (Vigil)* (see Chapter 3).

In May 1978, the Laboratory Theatre went to Gdansk. This was the company's first paratheatre tour within Poland and it is significant that it happened in the birthplace of the **Solidarity** movement (see later). The next major development in the paratheatre work was the opening of an event called *Tree of People* in January 1979. By this time, however, Grotowski's involvement in paratheatre activities was minimal. Since the University of Research, Grotowski's interests had begun to shift and in June 1978, he mentioned his new project by name for the first time— Theatre of Sources.

PARATHEATRE: SOME CONCLUSIONS

It is easy to criticize the Laboratory Theatre's foray into paratheatre by pointing out its naïveté and mysticism; formlessness and retreat from reality; and amateur techniques and lack of analysis. However, the reverberations from the experiment on a generation of young people cannot be denied. Participants, such as Margaret Croyden (Croyden 1993) and Steven Weinstein (cited in Kolankiewicz 1978: 77–82), reported a heightening of awareness, a harmony of effort and energy, a seldom-experienced vitality, a deep connection to nature, and the tangible stripping away of social and personality masks. Richard Mennen wrote in his journal after a *Special Project*: "I felt in my body ... something strong, hidden, like birth, like sex, like death; frightening and necessary. I do not know what it was, but it was something. It was also like a source" (Mennen 1975: 69).

Critics, such as Antoni Słonimski (cited in Osiński 1986: 156) and others who attended a symposium on paratheatre in Wroclaw in 2002, indicate that while participants often experienced something extraordinary, there was no reintegration process when they returned to their everyday lives. (This was especially strong for the Polish participants who had to go back to a harsh political and social reality.) Reports of depression and helplessness after a paratheatre experience bring up the question: Wouldn't it be better for young people to occupy themselves in the political or social fields rather than escape to the forest for a week? However, perhaps the glimpse of something "beyond" that

Grotowski's paratheatre experiments offered is exactly what everyone, and especially Grotowski's countrymen, needed in order to challenge themselves to effect change. Many participants kept the experience in their hearts as a precious memento, a utopian ideal momentarily made concrete and possible to work toward again. In this sense, as the experience of a generation, Grotowski's Theatre of Participation accomplished a great deal.

THEATRE OF SOURCES (1976–82)

From 1971 to 1976, Grotowski devoted much of his time to traveling around the world. Simultaneously, he was dealing with the developments of the paratheatre experiences led by different members of the Laboratory Theatre, with the controversies aroused by his "exit" from the theatre, and with his own deep intuitions. The next phase of his research, Theatre of Sources, grew out of Grotowski's nomadic experience and his personal search for cultural and spiritual roots. In 1974, in Paris, he delivered an address entitled, "The Theatre of Contact, Meeting and Roots." **Roots** is a term in Grotowski's lexicon that is synonymous with the words **source** and **origin**. Roots should not be understood as simply one's ethnic or cultural background, but its meaning goes beyond those limits to the roots of humanity itself: the true origin. Grotowski's paratheatre period was dedicated to the investigation of contact and meeting, but the principle of **roots** becomes essential in the development of Theatre of Sources. Grotowski's agenda was no longer hidden.

THE ART OF THE BEGINNER/TECHNIQUES OF SOURCES

Grotowski conducted his research with a small, international group at Brzezinka (Figure 1.6) through summer 1979. For the Theatre of Sources team, Brzezinka's workspaces, both outdoors and indoors, became a "theatre." But it was a *theatre* where only action took place, not acting. "In our investigation the orientation is naturally performative, active, looking for and not at all cutting the contact with what is around us or face to us" (Grotowski 1997b: 261). The work was very solitary, working "alone together," and in relationship with the natural environment. Grotowski's search with this transcultural group was for how to

Figure 1.6 Brzezinka (2003). Photographer unknown, courtesy of the Archive of the Grotowski Centre, Wroclaw

transform solitude into energy or force. They tried to develop personal **techniques of sources, techniques of the beginning**. They looked for those simple **actions** or **doings** that precede the differences of tradition, culture, or religion. If one considers yoga, Native American shamanism, or Dervish whirling techniques of sources, then Grotowski was seeking the sources of techniques of sources.

Often the doings were very simple and unsophisticated: to walk slowly, to run, to climb a tree. For Grotowski, temporarily suspending the body's daily-life habits often meant a return to simple, childlike movement. This movement is accomplished in a high state of attention: the organism is awake, alert, and the senses of seeing and listening function in conjunction with moving. In fact, moving itself becomes perceiving. Grotowski calls this state **"movement which is repose."** The term comes from the **Gnostic** *Gospel of Thomas* and is also mentioned in certain Tibetan yoga texts (Grotowski 1997b: 263). Grotowski believed that the movement which is repose may be the vital point where different techniques of sources begin.

> **Gnosticism**: is the doctrine of a wide range of religious sects in the early Christian era which teaches that freedom from matter (the body) comes through attainment of spiritual truth or gnosis (knowledge). The *Gospel of Thomas* is a collection of sayings of the resurrected Jesus, discovered in 1945, that have a distinct Gnostic point of view.

The Theatre of Sources team worked from what Grotowski calls their personal preferences, not the preferences of a particular tradition. This is true even though several members of the Theatre of Sources team were masters of a particular technique and everyone maintained strong links to their cultural heritage. The initial doings or propositions were then tested by other members of the group who approached them with different mind structures, different conditionings. If the proposition functioned for these others, the action would continue to get worked until something even more elementary appeared. In time, the simple doing would develop into a technique. Grotowski was applying many of the same principles of elimination as in his theatre work.

EXPEDITIONS

Part of the Theatre of Sources research involved making contact with authentic techniques of sources. Between July 1979 and February 1980, Grotowski and his Theatre of Sources team took a series of five expeditions to places where cultures still practiced techniques of sources: Haiti, Nigeria, Eastern Poland, Mexico, and India. Each expedition had its own unique qualities and organization. For the team members who participated, they were life-changing and life-affirming experiences.

The first step on the expedition was to make contact with people from the host countries and to select local participants for the team. The next step, the expedition itself, was to find a relation with the traditional practitioners or, in some cases, only their place of practice, their natural environment. Each expedition included Grotowski himself and a different constellation of team members. The first expedition traveled to Haiti, the home of the **voodoo** cult in its purest form.

> **Voodoo**: the ancient religion brought from Africa to the Americas. In its Caribbean form it mingles animism and Christian elements. Voodoo permeates all aspects of life in Haiti – its art, politics, education, and religious rituals.

In Haiti, Grotowski says the emphasis was on "witnessing some performative approaches [to ancient tradition] and on possibilities for entering into direct contact with the strong human examples of the holders of ancient tradition" (Grotowski 1997b: 269). Grotowski stresses that they did not go to Haiti to participate in voodoo, although the group did witness several authentic voodoo rituals. Grotowski's main contact was with the artistic community **Saint-Soleil**.

> **Saint-Soleil**: was a commune of peasant artists, created under the direction of **Jean-Claude (Tiga) Garoute (1935–2006)** and **Maud Robart (b. 1946)**. The group's unique primitive style of painting dazzled French writer Andre Malraux (1901–76) when he visited Haiti in 1975, and he devoted a chapter to them in his memoirs, bringing them to world attention. Saint-Soleil disbanded after several years, but the artistic style and movement continues. Tiga Garoute and Maud Robart worked with Grotowski over a period of years in Theatre of Sources and Objective Drama. Maud Robart continued her collaboration until 1993, assisting Grotowski in Italy during the final phase of his resgearch.

Grotowski then traveled to Nigeria accompanied solely by a Haitian colleague, a *hougan* (a voodoo priest). Together they visited Ifé, the cradle of the voodoo tradition. The third expedition journeyed to several remote villages in eastern Poland on the border with Byelorussia. The team then went to Mexico where the work "concentrated on psycho-ecological aspects of **Huicholes** culture: the notion of 'sacred, charged spots', and on performative possibilities related to these kinds of places" (Grotowski 1997b: 269).

> The **Huicholes**: are a tribe that has lived for centuries isolated in the Sierra Madre Mountains of Mexico. They have no word for "god," but worship the wonders of their natural environment. They believe that when humans destroy nature, they destroy the finest part of themselves. The Huicholes are a peyote-smoking tribe, but Grotowski and his group strictly avoided any involvement with this aspect of their culture.

The final expedition was to India, primarily the Bengal region, where the team made contact with members of the **Bauls**.

> The **Bauls**: are a cult of minstrels known for their ecstatic worship and unconventional modes of behavior. The word *baul* is derived from *batul*, meaning "beaten by the winds" or "mad." A clear representative of Grotowski's *yurodiviy* (holy fools), the Bauls belong to no caste and wander freely. The simple language of their songs, fervent rhythms, and sensuous dances are actually "a technique for seeking God in oneself by using the instrument of the body that God gave us" (Reymond 1995: 294).

On each expedition, Grotowski's Theatre of Sources diligently avoided exploiting these traditional cultures or appropriating elements of their rituals. Instead, the group simply made contact, kept a natural distance, and worked "next to" or in some relation with the traditional practitioners or their natural environment. Some individuals from the local cultures did eventually join Grotowski's team, and members of the Bauls and Saint-Soleil traveled to Poland in the summer of 1980 for the next phase of Theatre of Sources, which involved opening the work to the public under the title *Mysteria Originis*. Over three months, approximately 220 people participated in the activities of Theatre of Sources and the visiting traditional practitioners at Brzezinka and another nearby rural setting. Occurring at the same time, but separate from *Mysteria Originis*, were presentations of *Tree of People* and the final performances of *Apocalypsis cum figuris*. At the end of the summer, Grotowski disbanded the Theatre of Sources team and the members returned to their home countries.

THE POLISH CRISIS

While Grotowski conducted his fieldwork around the world and in isolation in Brzezinka, Poland was in turmoil. In October 1978, **Karol Wotyla (1920–2005)**, a Polish cardinal, was elected Pope. He took the name John Paul II and triumphantly returned to Poland in June 1979. His trip offered a whiff of hope to the oppressed Polish population and was followed by a month of workers' protests in December. Poland's economic problems worsened. The country was mired in debt and suffered severe food shortages throughout 1980, the year of the Theatre of Sources public opening.

At this time, **Lech Walesa (b. 1943)**, a shipyard worker, cofounded the labor union **Solidarność (Solidarity)**, with some fellow workers. Soon the organization numbered 10 million members. In August 1980, Walesa led the Gdansk shipyard strike which gave rise to a wave of work stoppages across much of the country. Pope John Paul II sent a message of support to the workers and the government authorities were eventually forced to relent. The Gdansk Agreement, signed on August 31, 1980, gave Polish workers the right to strike and to organize their own independent union.

In early 1981, **General Jaruzelski (b. 1923)** came to power. The tensions in Poland escalated and the unstable economic situation deteriorated. Solidarność made further demands, including democratic local governments. Soon after, the Soviet Union sent troops to begin training exercises inside of Poland. It seemed that Poland's attempts at reform would be quashed before they had even been born. On December 13, 1981, Jaruzelski imposed martial law and Solidarność was declared an illegal organization. Walesa and other union leaders were arrested and imprisoned and Poland descended into a dark winter of despair.

GROTOWSKI'S DILEMMA

During the period prior to martial law, Grotowski traveled throughout Poland, often incognito, talking to people, taking the pulse of his country. Meanwhile, the Laboratory Theatre opened a new performance in February 1981. *Thanatos Polski*, directed by Ryszard Cieślak and featuring actors from the original ensemble as well as members of the paratheatre team, unabashedly alluded to Poland's precarious political situation.

In early spring, Grotowski called certain members of the Theatre of Sources team to resume work, and a major Laboratory Theatre project was carried out in Sicily. When they returned to Poland, *Thanatos Polski*, *Tree of People*, and *Theatre of Sources (II)* were presented throughout the crisis summer of 1981 in Wroclaw and Brzezinka. The Theatre of Sources team also toured to several Polish villages during this period. The new version of Theatre of Sources included both indoor and outdoor work. The indoor work took the form of **individual actions** (see Chapter 4) performed by several members of the transcultural group and organized by Grotowski to be witnessed by the people of each village.

There followed a series of major personal and historic events which influenced Grotowski's future plans. Antoni Jahołkowski, one of the founding members of the Laboratory Theatre, died in September 1981 after a long illness. When martial law was declared in December, Grotowski was in Brzezinka working with the Theatre of Sources team. Ludwik Flaszen informed them of the crisis and the entire group immediately relocated to the theatre building in Wroclaw. The international participants were given the option to leave Poland. The few who stayed spent a meager, surreal Christmas garrisoned with Grotowski in the Wroclaw space, standing in long lines for the rationed food and supplies, dancing to the music of Supertramp, and watching with dread the tanks in the town square.

Grotowski prepared himself to be arrested. Other members of the intelligentsia and artistic community had already been incarcerated, and although he had not joined Solidarność because of his position as director and administrator, he knew that his activities were always under suspicion by the authorities. Each knock on the door set off a wave of reactions in the small group. The police, however, never came. Theatre companies from around the world offered their help and sent care packages to the Laboratory Theatre. Eventually, Grotowski was able to negotiate a trip to Denmark in January 1982 to visit Eugenio Barba.

On February 4, 1982, Jacek Zmysłowski died in New York City. He had become ill after the expedition to Haiti and was diagnosed with leukemia. His death hit Grotowski hard. They had developed a strong master–apprentice bond and Zmysłowski had become a vital part of Grotowski's continuing research. Grotowski changed radically after Zmysłowski's death. A new openness and softness appeared in his relations with others. He became more tolerant—and sad. Perhaps it was during this series of crises in 1981 and 1982 that Grotowski enacted another transformation. At the age of 48, he suddenly became an old man.

FAREWELL TO POLAND

By spring, Grotowski was able to arrange for the Theatre of Sources team to leave Poland. They installed themselves in Italy. From March through June 1982, Grotowski delivered a series of lectures about the organic process at the University of Rome and conducted practical work at a farm in Umbria.

In the summer, Grotowski returned to Poland with several members of the Theatre of Sources team. Although there was a faint-hearted effort to continue working, the situation in Poland proved impossible for Grotowski. The Jaruzelski government tried desperately to use artists to curry international favor. Grotowski, however, saw a big ethical difference between directing plays for a national audience under an oppressive regime, as many of his contemporaries chose to do, and using that same regime's money to operate a closed, international laboratory as was his wont. He knew that he could not maintain the work's pureness and his own integrity under the conditions of martial law. In September 1982, the Theatre of Sources group left again for Italy. In October 1982, Grotowski went to Haiti to ponder his dilemma. By December 10, he had taken up residence at the home of his close friend, André Gregory, in New York. When he was certain that each of his Laboratory Theatre colleagues was out of Poland and safe from retaliation, he officially requested political asylum in the United States.

On December 31, 1982, Jairo Cuesta locked the door of the workspace in Volterra, Italy, where the Theatre of Sources team had continued its activities, and terminated the project. The Laboratory Theatre in Wroclaw continued to operate for several years, but the actors worked primarily outside of Poland. Finally, the founding members, with Grotowski's consent, formally suspended operations in 1984. Amid little fanfare, a major chapter of twentieth-century theatre ended.

OBJECTIVE DRAMA (1983–6)

AN AMERICAN ADVENTURE

The termination of the Polish Laboratory Theatre did not mean the demise of its ringleader and creative force. Grotowski, finding himself in strange new circumstances and unsure as to how to proceed, managed to arrange an optimum situation in order to continue his work. After a year of teaching at Columbia University in New York City, he was invited by **Robert Cohen** to join the faculty of the University of California-Irvine. UC-Irvine offered him a professorship, research monies, exclusive use of an old barn situated on the campus, and the promise of three years of work without interference. Funding from the Rockefeller Foundation and the National Endowment for the Arts, as well as other individual donors, was also forthcoming. After several meetings with students and appeals for interested participants in the Los Angeles area newspapers, Grotowski began work in UC-Irvine's Studio Theatre. In the fall of 1983, the Focused Research Program in Objective Drama, Grotowski's brief American adventure, was initiated.

Robert Cohen (b. 1943): American educator and director. He has written numerous books on theatre and acting and was founding Chair of the Drama Department at UC-Irvine.

Grotowski regarded Objective Drama as a transitional period. After leaving Poland, he felt alienated and cut off from his roots and most of his long-time collaborators. He had been through several major personal losses and his own health was again causing him anxiety. So he decided to put his attention to small details and began to work on certain elements of craft that had been neglected during Theatre of Sources and Paratheatre. The three years of the Objective Drama program at UC-Irvine proved to be a valuable training ground in the fundamental principles of professional performance work.

The term Objective Drama can be traced to two separate sources. The first is a distinction made between objective art and subjective art by **G.I. Gurdjieff**:

> Subjective art relies on a randomness or individual view of things and phenomena, and thus it is often governed by human caprice. "Objective Art," on the other hand, has an extra- and supra-individual quality, and it can thereby reveal the laws of fate and the destiny of man.

(Osiński 1991: 385–6)

Gurdjieff offers the pyramids as one example of objective art.

> **G.I. Gurdjieff (1877?–1949)**: Armenian-born spiritual leader who eventually settled in France and taught a system of attaining awareness and control over one's life. His writings include *Meetings with Remarkable Men* (1963).

The second source for the term "objective drama" was a notebook kept by **Juliusz Osterwa** where he discusses the relative "objectivity" of the various arts, placing architecture above music, painting, and literature. Osterwa then speculates: "Suppose theatre is like architecture. [. . .] Architecture is the most refined . . . moves the experts and the observers to a state of rapture—while it affects everyone in such a way that they are not even conscious of it" (cited in Osiński 1991: 386).

> **Juliusz Osterwa (1885–1947)**: renowned Polish actor and director who founded the Reduta Theatre, a model for Grotowski's Laboratory Theatre.

With these two great thinkers as his impetus, Grotowski began to formulate his new research question: What are the structures or tools that have an objective impact on the performer? Are there certain techniques, spaces, movements, vocal vibrations that affect the performer, transform his/her energy, allowing him/her to enter an organic stream of impulses, of life?

PRACTICAL WORK IN IRVINE

At UC-Irvine, the work began in late October 1983 with Tiga Garoute and Maud Robart from Haiti. They taught a small group of university students, including **James Slowiak (b. 1955)**, and several community participants, a cycle of Haitian songs and dances that included the *yanvalou*. The *yanvalou* is a ritual dance with a strong rhythm that incorporates a subtle undulation of the spine and a bending forward from the hips. All songs and movement structures were learned solely by imitation. There were no explanations or translations given. The two traditional practitioners would sing and the group would repeat, for hours at a time. Eventually, these songs and movement structures were organized into an activity named The River. Initially, Grotowski also conducted several voice work sessions and the group began to learn The Motions exercise (see Chapter 4). These early Irvine sessions took place on weekends and usually began in the evening until early morning.

By January 1984, the old barn had been renovated, with a sprung wooden floor installed and pale blue walls. A wooden yurt, a modern adaptation of a circular shelter used by Central Asian nomads, was constructed nearby. These two buildings stood adjacent to an open field on the outskirts of Irvine's campus. Once activities moved to the new site, outdoor work commenced. Grotowski initiated several of the participants in some of the "actions" developed during Theatre of Sources. These included The Slow Walk and The Fast Walk.

Eventually, each day's work consisted primarily of The River, The Motions, Watching (see Chapter 4), and work on individual actions. The Haitian practitioners left Irvine after the first year. Other traditional specialists worked with the Irvine group for shorter periods of time. They included a dervish (who taught whirling) and a Japanese Zen priest (who taught karate). The group was soon joined by a Korean performer, a Balinese actor, a dancer from Taiwan, and Jairo Cuesta. In summer 1984, students arrived from Yale University and New York University for two 14-day workshops. Among the students was Thomas Richards.

In the third year of the Irvine project, Grotowski selected a performance team for more intensive work. Thomas Richards, Jairo Cuesta, and James Slowiak were part of this team. The result was an elementary performance structure called simply *Main Action*, which incorporated some of the Haitian songs, individual actions, and texts from ancient sources. *Main Action* told a simple story of initiation and served as a challenge to the team's capacity to work craft elements on a professional level.

OBJECTIVE DRAMA: SOME CONCLUSIONS

During the three years of the Objective Drama program at UC-Irvine, there were a number of open sessions for interested participants. Several of these lasted at least 36 hours. In May and June 1986, witnesses observed the work of the performance team, including

Main Action, in a session lasting about eight hours. Robert Cohen, André Gregory, and **Jan Kott** were among the witnesses.

> **Jan Kott (1914–2001)**: a renowned Polish theatre critic and theoretician who lived in the United States since 1966. His book *Shakespeare Our Contemporary* (1965) influenced a generation of stage directors.

In the three years of Objective Drama, several aims were accomplished: The Motions and Watching were structured and refined as significant new exercises; the Haitian songs and *yanvalou* became important tools for Grotowski's continuing research; and a young generation of actors and directors were introduced to the rigors of work on craft. But perhaps the most significant accomplishment of the Objective Drama program was that Grotowski met Thomas Richards and began a work of transmission that carried on until the end of his life.

OBJECTIVE DRAMA: ADDENDUM

Objective Drama was only one part of Grotowski's work in Irvine. During the school year 1985–6, Grotowski conducted an acting class for UC-Irvine students, assisted by James Slowiak. The class was completely outside of the parameters of the Objective Drama program and focused on the playing of a precise score of physical actions, establishment of a creative and personal framework for each scene, and tempo-rhythm.

Each year between 1987 and 1992, Grotowski returned to Irvine for two-week sessions with UC-Irvine students, always assisted by James Slowiak. In 1989, James Slowiak worked for five months with a group of students prior to Grotowski's arrival. In 1992, he and Jairo Cuesta worked with students from Irvine and The University of Akron as well as members of **New World Performance Laboratory**. The work from these sessions was witnessed and analyzed by Grotowski each time.

> **New World Performance Laboratory**: an ensemble and research theatre located in Akron, Ohio and codirected by James Slowiak and Jairo Cuesta. The group presents performances and workshops internationally.

Grotowski made clear that this more performance-oriented aspect of his work was completely separate from his personal research and did not in any way indicate his return to theatre. He regarded these Irvine sessions as "lessons in theatre craft—the work of the stage director with the actor—'in the old, noble sense, as in the remote times of Stanislavsky'" (cited in Schechner and Wolford 2001: 293). Grotowski had been diagnosed in 1985 with cancer. From that point on, his mission to transmit his knowledge and finish his work took on an urgent dimension.

RITUAL ARTS OR ART AS VEHICLE (1986–99)

When Grotowski began to feel pressure from his American allies to turn out a product, he moved his main activities to Italy at the invitation of **Roberto Bacci** and **Carla Pollastrelli**. Accompanying him as assistants on the new project were **Pablo Jimenez (b. 1956)**, Thomas Richards, and James Slowiak. In August 1986, they took up residence in Pontedera, in the heart of Tuscany, where a new workspace was prepared for the group on an old tobacco farm and vineyard about five kilometers outside of town.

> **Roberto Bacci (b. 1949)** and **Carla Pollastrelli (b. 1950)**: Italian theatre impresarios who often offered refuge to Polish groups during the 1980s. Their center in Pontedera continues to host the Workcenter of Jerzy Grotowski and Thomas Richards.

Selection sessions for long-term participants were held throughout August and September. Hundreds of young artists streamed to Pontedera over the next few years to participate in this new project. Grotowski and his team met them with a violent force. Grotowski informed his team that since they lacked any real professional skills, they must attack the participants like kamikazes. The three assistants took him at his word. Work sessions often lasted until dawn. Singing, physical training, and exercises on the fundamentals of craft were all part of the regimen. Grotowski had a vendetta against dilettantism and knew that he could not pursue his goals until the group could work at a high professional level. Grotowski watched the work and then met with each of the three assistants, coaxing them toward more precision and more quality in everything they did. Meanwhile, he continued to work in private sessions with Thomas Richards.

Grotowski was entering what he would call Art as Vehicle or Ritual Arts, the final phase of his research. This phase had two primary themes: **transmission** and **objectivity of ritual**. Transmission revealed itself most strongly in Grotowski's relationship with Thomas Richards. After a bumpy trial period, which he describes in his book *At Work with Grotowski on Physical Actions*, Richards dedicated himself to the tasks Grotowski set for him and met each challenge. Ultimately, Grotowski entrusted to Thomas Richards the heritage of his research.

"Objectivity of ritual" describes Grotowski's attempt to create a performative structure that functions as a tool for work on oneself. This structure is not aimed at a spectator, but is only for the persons doing it. The structure provides a detailed key for energy transformation—to ascend toward more subtle energy and reach a state of organicity: "the elements of the Action are the instruments to work on the body, the heart, and the head of the doers" (Grotowski 1995: 122). Grotowski and Thomas Richards accomplished this goal in the creation of an opus titled simply *Action* (see Chapter 3).

ANOTHER BEGINNING

Throughout the 1990s hundreds of theatre groups and other specialists journeyed to Pontedera to witness the Workcenter of Jerzy Grotowski's work and share their own productions and methods. These meetings occurred without publicity and resulted in discreet, informal exchanges about craft with Grotowski and the members of his research team. Included among these visitors was famed Russian director **Anatoly Vasiliev (b. 1942)** who, after witnessing *Action*, claimed Grotowski as his spiritual and professional father. Hundreds of young people have traveled to selection sessions and other encounters conducted by Thomas Richards and the Workcenter's Associate Director **Mario Biagini (b. 1964)**. Today, the Workcenter tours the world to present its work in the field of Art as Vehicle as well as more spectator-oriented performance structures.

Anatoly Vasiliev (b. 1942): Russian stage director whose productions stirred Europe in the 1980s and 1990s. He directs a theatre school and performance center in Moscow.

Grotowski spent the 1990s in a swirl of new activity. He returned briefly to Poland to receive a special honor in 1992. He organized a major project in Brazil in 1996 and made several trips to the United States, including residencies at NYU, Northwestern University, Fordham University, and Bennington College. He also received several other honors including a MacArthur "Genius" Fellowship (1991). In 1996, he was appointed the first Chair of Theatre Anthropology in the prestigious Collège de France. He delivered ten lectures in Paris between March 1997 and January 1998 on the subject of "The organic line in theatre and ritual."

All of this work was accomplished while battling his debilitating health. Grotowski spent the last year of his life in seclusion in his apartment in Pontedera under the care of Thomas Richards and Mario Biagini. He died on January 14, 1999. Several months later, Grotowski's ashes were strewn on Mount Arunachala in his beloved India.

2

GROTOWSKI'S KEY WRITINGS

Grotowski's actual writings are few. The one book printed under his name, *Towards a Poor Theatre*, is primarily a collection of interviews, production and workshop notes, and commentaries by Ludwik Flaszen and Eugenio Barba. It includes only five pieces written by Grotowski himself out of fifteen articles in the book. He disliked putting his thoughts on paper, knowing that once something was in print, it was in danger of becoming a recipe or formula. Language, for him, was alive, always changing, and should never become petrified.

Grotowski insisted that his knowledge could only be transmitted through direct contact, one to one interaction. He privileged the oral tradition, especially a direct master–apprentice relationship. But he also understood the need for public confrontation to test the validity of his views and to avoid the trap of self-delusion. He resorted to writing if he felt it was time to clarify ideas and carry his thoughts to the next level of analysis and understanding.

Grotowski often edited and reworked his lectures or interviews and most of his published material over the last 30 years of his life is based on such public encounters. This "live" aspect is evident, as his writing does not always follow the prescriptions of good grammar, and often takes on a prodding tone, challenging, and brimming over with ideas. To be present at one of Grotowski's conferences was to be bombarded by a machine gun one moment and carried aloft by an eagle the next;

attacked viciously by a wolf and then nursed by a wryly grinning gnome. His writings emulate this experience.

Richard Schechner and others have criticized Grotowski for the control he exerted over the translation and dissemination of his written works (Schechner and Wolford 2001: 472). One can make many assumptions about his obstinacy in this domain: his experience with totalitarianism, his Roman Catholic tradition, his firm belief in the master–apprentice model. However, given the detailed precision of his theatre productions and the rare quality he achieved in everything he did, the desire to control his writings seems only natural. Grotowski understood that in the future he would be remembered and scrutinized primarily through his writings. He wanted to be certain that the written word did not mislead or distort his views, but reflected his real thoughts and practices in the best possible manner.

ENTERING GROTOWSKI'S WORLD

Irina Rudakova has identified four basic concepts that recur throughout Grotowski's career. They are **sacrifice**, **presence (hic et nunc)**, **totality**, and the "elimination of the breach between 'literal' and 'represented' actions . . ." (Rudakova 1999: 24). There may be some overlap in defining these four concepts, but together they equal **organicity**, which is the permanent concern that pervades all of Grotowski's work and research.

In order to navigate the terrain of Grotowski's ideas and the issues surrounding his work, certain premises must be acknowledged. One premise concerns **paradox**. If someone has trouble accepting paradox, they will have trouble accepting Grotowski's thought system and rhetoric.

Paradox: exists when a statement or a group of statements seems to contradict itself but may in fact be true.

Another premise concerns Grotowski's **trans–spiritualism**. He draws his ideas and vocabulary from many metaphysical sources including Hinduism, Taoism, Gnosticism, Buddhism, as well as the works of **Carl Jung**, **Meister Eckhart**, and G.I. Gurdjieff. Grotowski refers to these various thought systems, not to imitate them or create a synthesis, but in order to measure his own methods and ideas.

> **Carl Jung (1875–1961)**: Swiss psychiatrist who approached the human psyche by exploring dreams, art, mythology, religion, and philosophy.

> **Meister Eckhart (1260–1327/8)**: German theologian, philosopher, and mystic, tried for heresy, whose metaphysical writings, simple yet abstract, drew extensively on mythic imagery and have influenced numerous modern philosophers.

DIALECTIC: THE ORGANIC AND THE ARTIFICIAL

Critics, such as Jane Milling and Graham Ley (2001), often focus on the contradictions in Grotowski's theories. They point out that his movement between theatre and non-theatre, his use of theatre rhetoric when speaking about spiritual matters, and his use of spiritual language in the theatre realm reveal two opposing impulses never resolved. Although Grotowski often changed his vocabulary and explored a variety of belief systems (traditional and contemporary), he never really veered from his chosen path of research. At the end of his life, during his lectures at the Collège de France, he referred to this chosen path as "the organic line in theatre and in ritual," and compared it to the "artificial line," most often found in the performing arts. Is this a contradiction that needs to be reconciled? Or is it precisely the dialectic between the two—**organic** and **artificial**—that reveals the conclusions of a theatre master who has realized how to utilize the tools of his craft as a vehicle for personal transformation? Examining a selection of Grotowski's published works from the various periods of his research allows us to see how this dialectic between organic and artificial defined his investigations and created a new paradigm for performers to view their work.

"TOWARDS A POOR THEATRE" (1965)

"Towards a Poor Theatre" (first published in Polish, 1965; translated by T.K. Wiewiorowski, 1967) is Grotowski's seminal article. It is the first article in the book, *Towards a Poor Theatre*, and clearly introduces several of the fundamental concepts of the Laboratory Theatre's work during the period of Theatre of Productions. In the article, Grotowski defines two fundamental concepts: **poor theatre** and performance as an **act of transgression**. He also provides an initial discussion of such key principles as: *via negativa*, *conjunctio-oppositorum*, archetype, myth, and the translumination of the actor. His thoughts about the function of myth in contemporary theatre and society illuminate his mastery of psychology, history, and anthropology. The article ends with a very brief, but intimate, description of the director–actor relationship in the Laboratory Theatre (see Chapter 3).

Grotowski says that he arrived at the concept of poor theatre as the result of a long process trying to define what is distinctively theatre and after a detailed investigation of the actor–audience relationship. Grotowski demands that theatre seek how it is different from other categories of performance, especially television and film. The outcome of this questioning is a **poor theatre**—stripped of spectacle, makeup, and superfluous decoration—grounded in the belief that the personal and scenic technique of the actor is the core of theatre art: "Theatre can exist without make-up, without autonomic costumes and scenography, without a separate performance area (stage), without sound effects and lighting, etc. It cannot exist without the actor–spectator relationship of perceptual, direct, 'live' communion" (Grotowski 2002: 19).

Grotowski's Poor Theatre is best understood in relation to his ideas about the Rich Theatre, a theatre "rich in flaws" (Grotowski 2002: 19). The Rich Theatre draws extensively from other disciplines and incorporates technical elements of cinema and video onto the stage. Instead of looking for what is unique about the theatre experience, the Rich Theatre defines theatre as a synthesis of other art forms and depends on the expansion and exploitation of technology and mechanical resources within the stage and auditorium. Grotowski and his collaborators, however, eschewed such "riches" and instead designed a new performance space for each production, including only the necessary elements.

Archetype/myth

When Grotowski began work on a playscript, he first tried to identify and confront the **archetype** in each text he directed. **Archetype**, for Grotowski, refers to the basic human situation in the text. Sometimes he referred to it as the **myth** itself. Grotowski's fear that language could freeze an organic process, often led him to use several terms to refer to the same concept or principle. In "Towards a Poor Theatre," he cites other terms, from the great humanists, that might substitute for archetype: roots, mythical soul, and group imagination (Grotowski 2002: 24).

Grotowski carefully analyzed the problem of myth in the history of theatre and in relation to other fields of knowledge, especially psychology and anthropology. He felt that traditionally myth had been used to liberate the "spiritual energy" of the congregation or tribe, as the spectator identified with the myth and became aware of his own personal truth in the truth of the myth. Grotowski realized that this traditional mythic form does not function in today's theatre, where spectators are less defined by tribal and religious beliefs, and the fear and pity that previously led an audience to catharsis no longer provokes response.

Grotowski proposed a **confrontation** with myth rather than identification. If the actors and director retain their personal associations and private experiences while attempting to incarnate the myth (or archetype) in performance, then the connection to the roots, and both the relativity of today's problems and the relativity of the roots, become perceivable for the spectator. In this struggle or confrontation, it is possible to touch a more personal, intimate layer in the actor, which when it is exposed elicits a shock that can crack both the actor's and the spectator's life-mask and touch each of them on a deeper level. Grotowski believed that, given the absence of a common belief system, it was only in the direct connection between actor and spectator, without artifice, in "the perceptivity of the human organism," that myth could allow us once again to experience a universal human truth.

Transgression and blasphemy

Looked at in this way, performance becomes an **act of transgression**, not in the sense of sinning, but in the sense of going beyond one's limits. What does that mean for the actor? Grotowski's language here becomes harsh. He speaks of taboo, of violation, but what he is asking really is for the theatre to reject its own clichés and to reassert itself as a place of provocation where we are able "To cross our frontiers, exceed our limitations, fill our emptiness—fulfill our selves" (Grotowski 2002: 21).

Grotowski recognizes his own fascination for the traditions and myths of his culture and nation, as well as his desire to attack them, to blaspheme. **Blasphemy** is not just parody or profanation, but for Grotowski means to challenge really those engrained traditions and myths (both cultural and religious) by taking measure and assaulting them with one's own experiences, which are, of course, determined by the collective experience of the time.

We can perhaps understand this kind of blasphemy better with an example. Let's suppose we are doing a performance about American soldiers. The common myth is the American soldier as liberator, hero, patriot, and protector of the unfortunate. Recent experience proves otherwise. We know American soldiers who are sadists, torturers, racists, and addicts. We know American soldiers who are schoolyard bullies, cowards, and questioners. The truth of the American soldier is much more complex than the myth, even though the myth is grounded in some kind of truth as well. The smiling American GI passing out chewing gum is a concrete memory for thousands of Italians from World War II. But if she reveals the underbelly of the myth, if she blasphemes, the actor provokes a response in the spectator that, after the initial shock, can allow us to reconsider our roots and the stories or myths we accept. We become brothers and sisters, sharing the shame or blame, exposing the secrets in the family closet. We become Grotowski's spectator-friend discussed in Chapter 1.

Via negativa and the beginning

In order for any of this to occur, the actor (and director) must be in a state of **passive readiness**, "a state in which one does not *want to do that* but rather *resigns from not doing it*" (Grotowski 2002: 17). This state is achieved by conscious application of the *via negativa*, where the actor's psychophysical blocks are systematically eradicated through the rigors of physical and vocal training and through creative work on the role. Grotowski underlines here that this process takes many years and is not voluntary. Yes, one must employ "concentration, confidence, exposure, and almost disappearance into the acting craft" (Grotowski 2002: 17), but all of this only brings one to the beginning of the road, a state of "passive readiness."

At this point, skeptics may start to bellow: What's so great about being in the beginning? Why privilege the beginning? And, once you are in the beginning, then what? Grotowski's answer: to be in the beginning is precisely where one wants to be. That is the point. The whole point. The act of transgression. And he clearly states it here in his first written article. It is in the state of the beginning, which Grotowski refers to here as a **technique of the trance**, where the actor's powers of body and mind become integrated and "emerge from the most intimate layers of his being and his instinct, springing forth in a sort of **translumination**." "Translumination" (a word made up by Grotowski) means moving toward a radiant, lucid, and inspiring state of being.

TECHNIQUE OF TRANCE: A DETOUR

Later, we will discuss further Grotowski's ideas about "the beginning." But perhaps it's now necessary to clarify Grotowski's use of the term **trance**. Strange notions of trance from Hollywood movies of zombies or phony hypnotists permeate popular culture. However, when Grotowski uses the term trance, he is applying it specifically to the arena of the performer, awareness of the partner, and the ability to adapt to one's surroundings.

> Let's say that we see an actor, during a performance, and what he is doing is very clear, clean, the organic process is visible, there is no disorder, everything arrives in an evident and strong manner; it's strong because it sends a kind of suggestion. We can say that it hypnotizes the people. At this moment, many people that are watching see something that is unknown, which is not only organicity and articulation. There is something more, a potent energetic phenomenon, and so people say: "this actor is in a state of trance."

(Grotowski 1982: 9–10, trans. mine)

For Grotowski, trance is the ideal state of an actor in performance. Trance (as a potent energetic phenomenon) exists when a different kind of consciousness appears. This "other" consciousness, more awake, more alert than the normal consciousness, involves a perceivable change of energy. Grotowski calls it a "transparent consciousness." Can the "organic process" exist without trance? Yes, but Grotowski points out that in such cases the reactions are not immediate because they must first pass through the actor's thought center. One of Grotowski's enduring searches was for the reduction of this breach between thought and action.

He observed that such integration occurs in trance states and each rehearsal or performance should provide the possibility for the performer to achieve this heightened state of awareness and alertness. There is no trick. Just as in ritual, trance occurs in Grotowski's world with repetition of a precise score of actions.

However, Grotowski makes a distinction between healthy and unhealthy trance. In a "healthy trance," the state of alertness is very high, and this new **transparent consciousness** perceives simultaneously, outside and inside, but perceives without either identification or becoming attached to anything. In this state, it is not "you" who reacts but it is "that" (the other consciousness) that reacts. This transparent consciousness gives the impression that time slows down, but the reactions are not slow in time, they are immediate. Conversely, in an "unhealthy trance," all awareness is lost. Grotowski often said that one way to test if someone is in a healthy trance is to throw something in front of them. If they avoid the obstacle, they are in a healthy trance. If they trip, the trance is unhealthy. In other words, an unhealthy trance is not a trance at all because awareness is not functioning.

Another quality of the transparent consciousness, is that, when it does not occur in an inter-human situation, it becomes "spatial." This "spatialness" may be difficult to assimilate for Westerners because it is not a space delimited by objects. Rather it is a space that contains all objects, not only physical objects, but also interior objects, like thoughts, emotions, and images.

And where is the body in such a space? In the transparent consciousness. And what happens if there is action? The body moves and reacts in a precise manner inside the transparent consciousness. In such a state, Grotowski claims that it is even difficult to say: "I move." One can say: "it moves" or even just say "there is movement." "Then at that moment, *movement is at the same time repose*. The movement and the body are inside the transparent consciousness . . . 'that' stays in repose and is spatial" (Grotowski 1982: 84). This spatialness becomes the witness or, if you prefer, the transparent consciousness becomes a spatial and serene witness. Several of these concepts (witness, movement in repose) will be developed further in Grotowski's Theatre of Sources and Ritual Arts phases of research, but perhaps we can bring these ideas to a more concrete level for the actor by comparing this "transparent consciousness as witness" to what Grotowski called the **secure partner** in Theatre of Productions.

Secure partner

In a 1967 interview with Richard Schechner, Grotowski discusses the secure partner and carefully outlines the actor's process in reaching the state of "giving oneself totally":

1. Begin with material that gives the actor a chance to explore his relationship with others.
2. Search for those memories or associations that have conditioned his contact with others.
3. The actor must give himself totally to the search and not play for himself or for the spectator.
4. The search must be directed from within himself **to** the outside, but not **for** the outside.
5. When the actor begins to live in relation to the partner from his own biography, he can start to use the other actors as screens for his life's partner. He projects his personal images and associations on to the characters in the play like on to a movie screen. He is reacting in the here and now to his partners, but he is also reacting to his personal score.
6. The final stage is that he discovers the "secure partner," this special being in front of whom he does everything, in front of whom he plays with the other characters and to whom he reveals his most personal problems and experiences.

(Grotowski 2002: 246–7; emphasis in the original)

In this interview, Grotowski states that the secure partner is a human being, but cannot be defined. He declares that a rebirth occurs in the actor, a visible change in his behavior, and that once the secure partner is discovered the actor is ready to resolve any creative problems he may encounter.

In the book *Towards a Poor Theatre*, Grotowski introduces several ideas about what he will eventually call the organic line of the actor. In these early articles, he calls it an inner technique, a spiritual technique, a personal process and he states categorically that "there is no contradiction between inner technique and artifice . . . ." In fact, it is through the artificial composition of a role (the form) that one discovers the spiritual line of the role. "The form is like a baited trap, to which the spiritual process responds spontaneously and against which it struggles" (Grotowski 2002: 17). In the next article selected, "Skara Speech," Grotowski elaborates on the actor's artificial line and some of the tools that can be used to assemble it.

"SKARA SPEECH" (1966)

"Skara Speech," also published in *Towards a Poor Theatre*, was delivered to a group of young workshop participants after a 10-day seminar at the Skara Drama School in Sweden in January 1966. Grotowski and his collaborators often conducted such seminars to introduce the physical and vocal exercises of the Laboratory Theatre. Although Grotowski never purported to teach a method, "Skara Speech" reads like an actor's primer. In this conversation on craft, Grotowski sets down several important acting concepts that go beyond any particular methodology:

- **Associations**   Associations cannot be planned. They are precise memories, which are not only thoughts, but are linked to the body and to the physical reaction of the memory. "It is to perform a concrete act, not a movement such as caressing in general but, for example, stroking a cat. Not an abstract cat but a cat which I have seen, with which I have contact. A cat with a specific name— Napoleon, if you like. And it is this particular cat you now caress. These are associations" (Grotowski 2002: 226).

- **Impulses**   Impulse is one of the most important concepts for the Grotowski actor. He often said that the way to perceive if an actor is working organically or not is to determine if he is working on the level of impulses. He also pinpoints his work on impulses as the major difference between his research and Stanislavsky's system of physical actions (Richards 1995: 99). In "Skara Speech" he mentions impulses numerous times, but he doesn't really define them. His definition comes much later in an interview in 1992:

> Before a small physical action there is an impulse. Therein lies the secret of something very difficult to grasp, because the impulse is a reaction that begins inside the body and which is visible only when it has already become a small action. The impulse is so complex that one cannot say that it is only of the corporeal domain.
>
> (cited in Richards 1995: 94)

Grotowski says that without impulse an action tends to stay on the level of gesture. The impulse is born inside the body, precedes the action, and pushes from the inside toward the periphery of the body, to become visible in the action. He told Thomas Richards that "impulses are the morphemes of acting . . . And the basic beats of acting are impulses prolonged into actions" (Richards 1995: 95). Grotowski also believed that training the impulses, even more than the physical actions, allows everything the actor does to become more rooted in the body.

How can one train the impulses? After you have a precise score of action—when you know what you are doing—you can begin to seek in your body the beginning point of the action. "One can say that the physical action is almost born, but it is still kept back, and in this way, in our body, we are 'placing' a right reaction (like one 'places the voice')" (Grotowski cited in Richards 1995: 95). You can train the impulses sitting on a bus in public. Movie actors often work impulses while waiting for their scene to be shot. It is the flow of impulses, coming from inside and moving unhindered toward the accomplishment of a precise action, which signifies Grotowski's notion of organicity.

- **Score** For Grotowski, a score—"clearly defined text and action"—is absolutely necessary for anything else to happen on stage. In performance, one should never look for spontaneity without a score. It is impossible. The score is your foundation as an actor. However, the score should not be confused with that sterile word so often heard in theatre—blocking. A score involves much more than just movement, it consists primarily of fixing the moments of contact between you and your partner(s).
- **Contact** Contact is one of the most essential elements of the actor's craft. Contact should not be understood merely as eye contact or staring fixedly at your partner. Contact is to really see. If you really see and listen to your partner, there is a natural adaptation which occurs. You must adjust what you are doing because today, even though you and your partner are following the same score of actions, there will always be slight differences. True improvisation happens on this level of seeing, listening, and adjusting—to be present and alive on stage is to be in contact and this contact results in harmony between you and your partner. You are both together in the same moment—seeing, listening, and responding.

Grotowski gives two exercises for working on contact. Both exercises demand that the score is already fixed—they should happen late in the rehearsal process, when the play is almost ready to be performed. In the first exercise, one actor is given the task to play in a radically different manner, while the others maintain their scores and yet adjust their reactions within their scores to the new stimuli. The second exercise involves two partners who play a scene and change their intentions, while still sticking to the physical score of action. The danger comes with the temptation, in both exercises, to alter the physical score. No, that is too easy. The actor must keep the physical score and renew the contact.

- **Sign** Grotowski's work with actors during the Theatre of Productions phase of his research was based on the construction of signs. A sign "is a human reaction, purified of all fragments, of all other details which are not of paramount importance. The sign is the clear impulse, the pure impulse. The actions of the actors are for us signs" (Grotowski 2002: 234).

Herein lays a great difference between Grotowski's work with actors and Stanislavsky's work on physical actions. Grotowski was not interested in reconstructing daily-life behavior on stage. He felt that so-called natural behavior was just another fabricated form that actually served to obscure the truth rather than reveal it. He points out that in an extraordinary situation (a moment of terror, joy or danger) a human being does not behave "naturally." "A man in an elevated spiritual state uses rhythmically articulated signs, begins to dance, to sing. A sign, not a common gesture, is the elementary integer of expression for us" (Grotowski 2002: 17–18).

It is interesting to note here that in Thomas Richards' book, the translation of this remark by Grotowski is changed to: "Not common gesture or daily 'naturality' but a sign is proper to our primal expression" (Richards 1995: 104). Later, Richards again substitutes the word "common" for "natural." We believe that in this new translation, Grotowski was trying to make the distinction between what is natural, organic, primal, and other daily-life, quotidian behavior modes. He was interested in what was natural, not in what was common or quotidian. The change also clarifies how signs occur as a part of one's natural expression and then can be worked as part of a formal technique in the theatre.

In Grotowski's theatre, the actor's role is constructed of signs through which impulses can flow. The sign becomes the exterior form that the spectator perceives. Grotowski's signs should not be confused with *mudras* from **Indian Kathakali** or Artaud's hieroglyphs. Signs do not comprise a vocabulary of movement. Signs arrive from distilling the actor's actions, "by eliminating those elements of 'natural' (common) behavior which obscure pure impulse" (Grotowski 2002: 18). The result for the actor is a fixed and formal score of signs that serves as a trap for the inner process and as a door to enter "the living stream of impulses" (Richards 1995: 104).

Indian Kathakali: a spectacular form of Indian dance-drama that originated in Kerala over 500 years ago. The actors wear vivid makeup and elaborate costumes and tell their stories using *mudras* (precise hand gestures), body movement, and facial expressions.

- **Cliché** In "Skara Speech," Grotowski warns actors against play-ing clichés—taking the "easy road of associations." For example, if you always say "What a beautiful day!" with a happy tone and "Today I'm a little sad," with a sad tone, you are simply illustrating the words and not revealing the complexity of the human being behind the commonplace words. The playwright's words should never be illus-trated. Perhaps the spectator is more content with these "beautiful lies," but the actor should not work to please or pander to the spectator. The actor's job is to tell the truth and "always try to show the unknown side of things to the spectator" (Grotowski 2002: 237).

One example Grotowski gives concerns the Madonna: If you have to play the Virgin Mary, the cliché would be a mother leaning tenderly over her baby. But motherhood is much more complicated. There is an aspect of "cow," milk-giver in mother. There is also the aspect of destroyer, like the Indian goddess Kali. A true depiction of the Madonna should reveal more than the beauty of motherhood, even if such a portrait is not popular.

- **Authenticity** Grotowski says, "Aim always for authenticity" (Grotowski 2002: 237). You cannot play death because you have not experienced death. But you can confront your fear when faced with death or suffering. You can remember your physiological reaction when you first saw a dead body or you can imagine your future death—but with a cruel honesty, really asking yourself, "How will I die?" Then the actor is penetrating his own experience in an authentic way, making a sacrifice.

What if you have to kill someone in a play? Most likely you have never killed anyone in your life, but you probably have killed something— a fly, a grasshopper, a mosquito. Try to remember the physiological process of stalking, of waiting, or the impulsive swat and the reaction to the blood. But if you have to kill an animal in a play, it is not enough of a challenge to remember killing an animal. It's no sacrifice. Perhaps instead you remember the thrill of a sexual encounter. Then in the moment when you are to kill the animal, you **substitute** the details of your lovemaking. Now you are entering the realm of great acting, where you are really approaching something personal and mysterious.

The actor works with what Grotowski calls **body-memory**. Grotowski says the body does not have memory, the body is memory. This differs from Stanislavsky's emotional memory or affective memory, because you are not remembering the emotion, but you are letting your body remember what you did—the precise details of the actions. With the body-memory, the actor works with past experiences, but as mentioned earlier in the example about dying, the actor can also work with possible futures. In these cases, it's more a question of body-future or body-need. Eventually, Grotowski gave up the term body-memory and began to refer to the **body-life**—that stream of impulses that guides us toward what we need, toward revealing all of the landscapes inside us, the open or closed spaces, the past, and the potential. The body-life is our authentic self, freed of blockages, and forms a direct link to what Grotowski will eventually call the **body of essence**.

- **Ethics**   Grotowski ends "Skara Speech" with a discussion of ethics for actors. He says that for him morality or ethics is "to express in your work the whole truth" (Grotowski 2002: 238). In order to do this there must be discipline and organization in the work. He advises actors to leave the social world outside the rehearsal hall and to give themselves totally to the work. He finishes with a warning against "publicotropism." Publicotropism occurs when an actor orients herself too much toward the public. Authenticity demands that the actor not work for the public's pleasure or adulation. Grotowski decries the kind of marketplace theatre that forces actors into prostituting themselves for the public and selling their own bodies.

Grotowski also discusses ethics in several other articles, especially in the "Statement of Principles," a text written for apprentices and workshop participants at the Laboratory Theatre. In this article, published in *Towards a Poor Theatre*, Grotowski delineates the strict code of behavior, risk-taking, and attitude toward one's work and one's self necessary to accomplish a "total act" –

> This act cannot exist if the actor is more concerned with charm, personal success, applause and salary than with creation as understood in its highest form. It cannot exist if the actor conditions it according to the size of his part, his place in the performance, the day or kind of audience. There can be no total act if the actor, even away from the theatre, dissipates his creative impulse and, as we said before, sullies it, blocks it, particularly through incidental engagements of a doubtful nature or by the premeditated use of the creative act as a means to further his own career.
>
> (Grotowski 2002: 262)

After the intense rigor and discipline of the Theatre of Productions and his often stern pronouncements, Grotowski's abrupt turn toward "Holiday" seems both surprising and utterly natural.

"HOLIDAY" [*SWIETO*] "THE DAY THAT IS HOLY" (1970, 1971, 1972)

> Some words are dead, even though we are still using them. Among such words are: show, theater, audience, etc. But what is alive? Adventure and meeting . . . For this, what do we need? First of all, a place and *our own kind*; and then that our kind, who we do not know, should come, too . . . . What is possible together? Holiday.
>
> (Grotowski 1997a: 215)

In this startling manner, Grotowski announced his retreat from the arena of theatre production and set forth the parameters of his paratheatre research. Even today his words spark heated debate among theatre artists.

The "Holiday" text is based on several public forums and first appeared in English in *The Drama Review* in June 1973. Grotowski reedited the article for inclusion in *The Grotowski Sourcebook* (1997). The differences between the two English versions reveal the path Grotowski's search took in the twenty odd years after seemingly turning his back on theatre. What appears most evident is that many of his most brutal pronouncements about the impending death of theatre were removed from the article. In the 1990s, he was much more open to the fact that he never really left the theatre. Yes, of course, he left the theatre of production, of doing plays, of openings and closings, and rehearsals in the conventional manner. But he always referred to himself as a stage director and never shunned the theatre craft itself. However, in the early 1970s he had to squelch forcefully the public's expectations that he would continue to stage performances.

The new version of "Holiday" retains several of Grotowski's edicts against theatre for monetary gain or public adulation and as a place to hide oneself, but it emphasizes more clearly the alternative path that he personally chose to explore. He calls this path "the need to find a meaning" and points out that it has existed in all epochs when "people are aware of their human condition." He compares the quest to the practices of early Christianity, yoga, and Buddhism. He describes it as "the quest for what is most essential in life . . . " And what exactly is that? Grotowski answers: "One can't formulate it. One can only do it" (Grotowski 1997a: 220).

The language and form of "Holiday" is very much of the times. The euphoric optimism of cultural change often associated with the early 1970s pervades many of Grotowski's affirmations. But Grotowski is quick to point out that he does not speak in metaphors. He speaks of experience, of actions, of doing. "This is tangible and practical. It is not philosophy but something one does . . . This has to be taken literally, this is experience . . . It is enough to understand that I am attempting here—in as much as I can—to touch on the experience of meeting—meeting with man [*człowiek*] . . . " (Grotowski 1997a: 219).

The concept of meeting has already been discussed (see Chapter 1). But in the new version of "Holiday," Grotowski clarifies his use of the word "man" with the Polish word *człowiek* (pronounced chwo-vyek). The Polish word has no gender association, but also cannot simply be defined as human being. For now, let's say that *człowiek* is the archetype that exists beyond gender, personality, identity, and social codes—when one has unveiled oneself. Therefore, the meeting that Grotowski seeks in "Holiday" could never occur in the carnival atmosphere of show business. Grotowski admits that the meeting has occurred already in his own rehearsal hall and even in performances of the Laboratory Theatre, but now he wonders if it can be extended beyond the confines of theatre altogether.

He declares the word "audience" dead. He wants to liberate the actor from slavery to the audience's approval. He also wants to liberate the audience. "Holiday" calls for a cleansing—to fling open the windows of the theatre and get rid of the pollution stifling the stream of life—both on stage and in each one's own daily life.

Grotowski never negates the fundamental contributions of his "father," Stanislavsky. He does, though, compare Stanislavsky's work in the theatre with the goals of his own work:

> What, for example, distinguishes what we are aiming at from Stanislavsky's wisdom, that genuine wisdom of craft? For us the question is: what do you want to do with your life; and so—do you want to hide, or to reveal yourself? There is a word which, in many languages, has a double meaning: the word *discover/uncover*. To discover oneself means to find oneself, and at the same time uncover what has been covered: to unveil.
>
> (Grotowski 1997a: 219)

Grotowski makes clear that his own quest takes him outside the conventions of theatre, but that if a written play, *Hamlet*, for example, is essential for someone else as a departure point, then work with Hamlet. But don't just play the character. Measure oneself with Hamlet. Measure your man (*człowiek*) with Hamlet's and don't lie about your own existence. What appears then is the "fullness of man," man in his totality, undivided, "I am as I am."

Grotowski also speaks to the questions of collective creation, talent, and audience. Collective creation, popularized in the 1960s and 1970s primarily through the work of the **Living Theatre**, struck Grotowski as just another kind of dictatorship. Instead of a single tyrant as director, the entire group interferes in the work of each member, most often resulting in compromise, barrenness, and half-measures. The answer for Grotowski does not lie in the method—one single director or a collective—but in the creation of an atmosphere where the actor is secure enough to reveal himself.

The Living Theatre: legendary American experimental theatre company founded in 1947 by Judith Malina (b. 1926) and Julian Beck (1925–85). The anarchic group gained recognition in the 1960s and 1970s with semi-improvisational collective creations that toured internationally and often performed in gnontraditional settings.

In terms of talent, Grotowski categorically states that "Talent as such does not exist, only its absence" (Grotowski 1997a: 225). When someone is doing something which does not fit him—this is lack of talent. As for the audience, Grotowski asks, "Why worry about what the audience's part ought to be?" (Grotowski 1997a: 225). Just do something and someone will come who wants to meet you.

Sincerity is the endpoint of "Holiday." Sincerity reveals that which is exclusively personal and, paradoxically, that which is the incarnation of the total man [*człowiek zupełny*]. This brings us to the controversial idea of a collective area of myth, a common source, the archetype mentioned earlier. Scholars, such as Richard Schechner (Schechner and Wolford 2001: 492), have questioned Grotowski's unfashionable insistence on a common origin, something universal and essential. In "Holiday," Grotowski states as a matter of fact that he is not interested in the discussion of whether or not such a thing exists or even how it exists. He believes, "That area [the common source] exists naturally, when our revelation, our act, reaches far enough, and if it is concrete" (Grotowski 1997a: 224). In Grotowski's world, order is never abandoned. Order and form give one the freedom to be as one is and operate as the banks and bed of the river through which the living waters flow: "I am water, pure, which flows, living water; and then the source is *he*, *she*, not *I*: he whom I am going forward to meet, before whom I do not defend myself. Only if *he* is the source can *I* be the living water" (Grotowski 1997a: 217; emphasis in the original). In "Holiday," Grotowski names this source as "brother"—that which is most essential. "This contains 'the likeness of god', giving and man [*człowiek*]. But also the brother of earth, the brother of senses, the brother of sun, the brother of touch, the brother of Milky Way, the brother of grass, the brother of river" (Grotowski 1997a: 221).

Is Grotowski's language here too precious? Too mystical? Too audacious? Perhaps. One can certainly quibble with Grotowski's semantics, with his science, his theology, or his vagueness. But today "Holiday" still resonates as the howl of a man seeking answers to the great existential question: "Where is my nativity—as brother?" (Grotowski 1997a: 225). This question, which ends the article "Holiday," brings us directly to Grotowski's next phase of research discussed in his text, "Theatre of Sources."

"THEATRE OF SOURCES" (1997)

In the three articles discussed so far, the relation of Grotowski's writings to theatre and the actor's craft is obvious. Even the anti-theatre tone of "Holiday" provides a touchstone for those actors working in the arena of public performance. But during Theatre of Sources, Grotowski veers directly into his hidden agenda and the deep personal questions that accompanied his life's work. Ronald Grimes points out that Theatre of Sources is less about "The Actor's Work *on* Himself" and more about "The Actor's Work *as* Himself" (Grimes 1981: 274). This is a major shift in direction and may leave some theatre artists struggling to see the value in Grotowski's rhetoric about knowing one's self and one's source.

Ludwik Flaszen says that the 1970s were the happiest time in Grotowski's personal life. Grotowski himself often referred to this period as the Belle Époque. Grotowski never married and never owned a house or apartment. For a brief time, he owned a blue Fiat 126 that barely could accommodate his long body. But he never drove a car— except once during a crazy moment in the Australian Outback with no other vehicle in sight. His colleagues were terrified. During Theatre of Sources, he gave away many of his personal belongings and even loaned his small state-owned apartment to a foreign member of the company to house his wife and daughter. Grotowski went to reside in an isolated room of the Laboratory Theatre building. When in Brzezinka, he lived under the same conditions as the rest of the group.

The version of "Theatre of Sources" that appears in *The Grotowski Sourcebook* is a compilation of fragments from several of Grotowski's texts and talks from between 1979 and 1982. The article gathers together some of his practical observations and reminiscences about this period of work. Grotowski starts with his own roots and process. He then passes to the process of the young people of "his kind," involved in the project, from different cultural and religious traditions, and then finally to his observations of practices of a whole community of "traditional religious" practitioners. He ends with what can only be assumed is a personal story of awakening.

The article begins as a confession. Grotowski reveals aspects of his own nativity, his own roots, and lays out the stimuli for the questions of his life's work. He tells about seeing a calf butchered for the first time, eavesdropping from under the table on the "babbling" of the adults, and his own battle with sickness and physical weakness. He recalls "craving organicity." He relates this craving to a need for a weapon, grounding, and a support for his ego. Some people may seek this grounding in attachment to a particular religion. Grotowski found his answer through exploring diverse traditions, refusing the concept of heaven or afterlife, and in accepting an orientation toward *hic et nunc* (the here and now).

He tells a story that took place in his village during the war, when he was about nine years old. Near his house, there was a wild apple tree that had a very particular shape. The tree attracted him. He would climb the tree and was sometimes possessed by the irrational temptation to do things in relation to the tree, almost as if he were the tree's priest. In fact, he would say a kind of Mass beside the tree. He was transported somewhere else.

Where is the "somewhere" he is talking about? He tries to clarify the paradigm that will frame his observations. He finds the roots of it in the old traditions introduced to him by his mother or by his own discoveries as a young boy: "When something like this happens to a human being, then—as they say in different traditions—'the imprint of the heart planes in the space'" (Grotowski 1997b: 253). The human awakes. Grotowski's hypothesis about awakening begins with a personal experience between him and an apple tree.

Grotowski organizes Theatre of Sources around the dialectics of the "beginning." For Grotowski "to be in the beginning" is a personal experience of "now" (*hic et nunc*). He asks the question: What is the daily practice of a person who confronts his own life questions in a manner not attached to any specific religion or culture? Is there a transcultural possibility? Is there a source technique that exists "before the differences?" In other words, what happens when one suspends the daily, habitual techniques of the body that differentiate cultures? What first appears is deconditioning of perception: "we are programmed in such a way that our attention records exclusively those stimuli that are in agreement with our learned image of the world. In other words, all the time we tell ourselves the same story" (Grotowski 1997b: 259). If this habitual perception is disrupted, new stimuli from outside can enter our field of attention. Our tamed body and mind can remember its forgotten, "untamed" nature. For Grotowski, it is like going back to a childlike state. A child who enters a forest for the first time takes nothing for granted. She is like the "man who precedes differences."

In his 1982 University of Rome lectures, Grotowski discusses the question of **mind structure**. Working with young people from different cultures and traditions (not all practitioners of an "old tradition"), Grotowski became aware of the diverse ways each one sees the world. A phenomenon or experience was seen, described, remembered, or understood differently by a Japanese, Hindu, Haitian, or Colombian. It depended on their mind structure. That was why Grotowski was interested only in actions, experiences that could be described, remembered, or understood in an objective way. The actions also needed to be dramatic or performative—"related to the organism in action, to the drive, to the organicity"—and ecological—"linked to the forces of life, to what we call the living world . . . to be not cut off (to be not blind and not deaf) face to what is outside of us" (Grotowski 1997b: 259). The Theatre of Sources team sought simple, primary actions, like just walking. After months of refining the "doings," the actions, team members would confront each other's work. At this point it became clear for Grotowski if the actions were working in the realm of "before the differences."

Grotowski's full vision of Theatre of Sources never came to fruition. Looking back, he saw that maybe Theatre of Sources is "just a premise for a field of work-possibility, remote in time; right now the point can be even a simple opportunity to meet some very special persons of tradition" (Grotowski 1997b: 268).

Critics, such as Milling and Ley (2001), have accused Grotowski of cultural appropriation during Theatre of Sources. These accusations do not really have any basis in fact. Grotowski acknowledged that any contact with a tradition will have some reverberation (positive and negative) for both groups. Grotowski also knew that the opportunity to connect with these source traditions was becoming increasingly rare as the monster of globalization encroached more and more on their territory. These cultures were changing and would continue to change—if his group made contact with them or not. He, therefore, kept the team's attempts at cognition very modest. They sought cognition that in no way disturbed the event; cognition which "in practice became almost transparent for persons whose culture, language, mental and behavioral habits, traditions and mind structures were extremely different" (Grotowski 1997b: 268). Often they just followed—no verbalization, no exterior imitation, in solitude next to the others, in silence while doing. A kind of battlefield solidarity was achieved as they worked individually among others. They just perceived: the flow of impulses, the circulation of attention, the awakening.

Grotowski finishes his article, "Theatre of Sources," with a personal recollection of awakening—not through the texts of other traditions— but through his own experience. A young actor might view this episode as a mirror of the process of **creativity**. Grotowski recounts a full and rich experience that becomes a journey toward the beginning: "Why was it so full? Maybe because a moment before you were asleep you were not lying to yourself that you know something. Maybe because you lost all hope" (Grotowski 1997b: 270). As an ancient text says: "Happy is he who stands in the beginning."

"TU ES LE FILS DE QUELQU'UN (YOU ARE SOMEONE'S SON)" (1989)

Midway through the Objective Drama Program, Grotowski conducted a two-month summer seminar in Tuscany. Thomas Richards participated in the workshop and describes it in his book, *At Work with Grotowski on Physical Actions*. "You are someone's son," one of Grotowski's most remarkable texts, is based on a talk he delivered in Florence and features many of his preoccupations during the summer of 1985. Grotowski had left Poland several years before and finds himself enmeshed in an American culture of consumerism and instant gratification. Everyone just wants to have "fun" and the word "work" has become anathema to young people in the 1980s. How does the old man Grotowski situate himself in this crazy world of yuppies and music videos? He does it by looking back, by embracing the past, the ancestors.

At first, Grotowski's text sounds like a political manifesto as he defends his relationship with art, with "social activity through culture," and with rebellion itself: "Bad artists *talk* about the rebellion, but true artists *do* the rebellion . . . Art as rebellion is to create the *fait accompli* which pushes back the limits imposed by society or, in tyrannical systems, imposed by power. But you can't push back these limits if you are not credible . . ." (Grotowski 1989: 295). Grotowski lambastes dilettantes, those who lack competence and precision in what they choose to do and never master their craft. Good intentions are no substitute for doing something well. "Real rebellion in art is persistent, mastered, never dilettante. Art has always been the effort to confront oneself with the insufficiency, and by this very fact, art has always been complementary to social reality" (Grotowski 1989: 296). Grotowski then redefines theatre as "all the phenomena around theatre, the whole culture" (Grotowski 1989: 296). What about those critics who maintain that theatre is only what happens on a stage in front of an audience with actors representing characters conceived by a playwright? Grotowski goes on to demonstrate how his research expands the boundaries of theatre and yet remains valuable for more conventional theatre practitioners.

Grotowski unleashes a ruthless analysis of the state of improvisation in the theatre. He lists the clichés of group improvisation: playing "savages" or monsters, imitating trances, forming processions, consoling a victim, drumming on the floor, using one's own daily-life behavior, etc. He then formulates an important principle: "Looking for connection, one should begin with disconnection" (Grotowski 1989: 296). In other words, use the space in such a way that your partner has the possibility to create. *Don't disturb the other*. When actors learn the ability to be "in disconnection," they are naturally in harmony. They are only seeing and listening and reacting. They are not imposing themselves, their own cleverness, or their own banalities on the others. But in order to begin to work on disconnection, a certain fundamental competence already must be attained on the level of movement, voice, and rhythm. Grotowski says that only then can work on improvisation be fruitful, not irresponsible, and only then, when mastery is achieved, do real questions of heart and spirit appear.

At this point in the text, Grotowski seemingly switches topics. Suddenly he is speaking as an anthropologist—a theatre anthropologist to be sure, but still an anthropologist. He describes the "primary position of the human body" found among hunters in Africa, France, Bengal, and Mexico—spine slightly inclined, knees slightly bent, the sacrum–pelvis complex engaged. Through a series of evocative images he links this *Homo erectus* position to the "reptile" aspect of humans: what the **Tantras** call the serpent asleep at the base of the spine; scientists refer to as the reptile brain; and which can even be seen in the development of the embryo. He describes how this position leads to a particular, rhythmic way of walking that serves to make the hunter silent and invisible to the animals. Grotowski relates this primary position, connected to the ancient body, to what he calls "primary energy" and he describes his search for techniques to access this energy. He found numerous examples in traditional cultures around the world, but discovered that these techniques were too sophisticated to be learned easily. However, Grotowski determined that in the derivatives of traditions, in Haiti for example, certain instruments or techniques to access primary energy are simpler and can be mastered artistically.

Tantras: a collection of mystical Hindu or Buddhist writings associated with the practice of Tantrism, a series of voluntary rituals which may include deity visualization, chanting, and focus on the body.

Grotowski calls these instruments *organons* (Greek) or *yantras* (Sanskrit). They function as precise tools, like a surgeon's scalpel or a navigator's compass, and can reconnect the doer with laws of nature. The primary position ("reptile body"), certain dances, like the *yanvalou*, and ritual songs from traditional cultures serve as *organons* or *yantras* in Grotowski's work. Grotowski asserts that these *organons* or *yantras*, when executed with competence, put the doer in a state of vigilance—where instinct and consciousness coexist in the same moment. The doer is simultaneously fully animal and fully human—

> ... in the true traditional techniques and in the true "performing arts," one holds these two extreme poles at the same time. It means "to be in the beginning," to be "*standing* in the beginning." The beginning is all of your original nature, present now, here. Your original nature with all of its aspects: divine or animal, instinctual, passionate.
>
> (Grotowski 1989: 300)

Grotowski reveals that it is the tension between these two poles that leads to totality in the doer—it makes man (*człowiek*). Here Grotowski defines *człowiek* as the quality which is "linked to the vertical axis, 'to stand'. In certain languages, to say man one says 'that which stands up'" (Grotowski 1989: 300). The identification of certain performative *organons* or *yantras* and the tedious process of learning them and executing them competently was the basis of Grotowski's work in Objective Drama.

Grotowski stresses that these *yantras* should not be used to make performances. They operate on the development of the individual in a potent manner and cannot be manipulated without distortion or phoniness. They are precise tools for the circulation of energy. He returns to the questions of dilettantism and the problems of chaotic improvisation versus what he calls **harmonic improvisation**, when the actor constantly readapts to a structure. He compares the modern actor to a tourist, always replacing one proposition with another, never accomplishing anything, working "sideways," not vertically. Grotowski describes the work on **ethnodramas** (see Chapter 4) in the Objective Drama program and how the individual must take responsibility for building, condensing, and editing his actions. He describes the arc of creation as always passing through phases of crisis followed by organicity, crisis, and then organicity—spontaneity of life followed by technical absorption.

Grotowski then explains how to work with a song of tradition in order to seek the primary energy, the appearance of the song, one's heritage, and one's human ties. He alludes to the fact that an actor can undertake such a process with any quality material, *Hamlet*, for example. Grotowski's account of the process of working on a song presages his work with Thomas Richards in the next few years. Grotowski enumerates the questions to ask yourself as you work. He gives a kind of road map to follow as you look for the song and the first singer of the song. Eventually, he says, you will discover that you come from somewhere—"It is you two hundred, three hundred, four hundred, or one thousand years ago, but it is you. Because he who began to sing the first words was someone's son, from somewhere, from some place, so, if you refind this, you are someone's son" (Grotowski 1989: 304).

Grotowski ends his analysis with the actor's classic question: is it me or is it the character? "But if you are the son of the one who first sang this song, yes, it is that which is the true trace of character. You are from some time, from some place. It's not a matter of playing the role of somebody who you are not" (Grotowski 1989: 304). In this extraordinary text, Grotowski provides actors with a guide, not a method or recipe, but certain principles to follow, for how to approach performance material and connect with its most human aspect: how to confront one's ancestors, how to improvise, how to work vertically. Once the question of competency is answered, "the question of you—of man [*człowiek*]" presents itself. "Are you man [*człowiek*]?"

(Grotowski 1989: 305). In his next text, "Performer," Grotowski offers a response to his own question.

"PERFORMER" (1988)

In March 1987, at a press conference in Florence to mark the opening of Grotowski's Workcenter in Italy and its connection with Peter Brook's International Center for Theatre Creation in Paris, Brook asked Grotowski a question: "Can you make more clear to us how and to what degree your work on dramatic art is inseparable from having around you people whose real need is for a personal inner evolution?" (Brook 1995: 384). Shortly thereafter, the Workcenter published a pamphlet which included Brook's text followed by what could be regarded as Grotowski's response: "Performer."

The genesis of "Performer" is very interesting. The text was born at the first public meeting about Grotowski's new phase of research in February 1987 in Pontedera. French critic Georges Banu took careful notes on Grotowski's remarks. Grotowski then reworked Banu's published notes into his own recollection of the talk and included a lengthy citation/montage from two sermons by Meister Eckhart. The entire process emulates Grotowski's process of oral transmission: a third person recollection is transformed by Grotowski into a first person text and then Grotowski himself as the third person in relation to Meister Eckhart quotes in the voice of Eckhart. With his editing of the text, Grotowski constructs a concise discourse on transmission; a final statement on the power and changeability of words and, as Ferdinando Taviani points out, what happens *between the words* (Taviani 1992: 265).

As he enters his final period of work, Grotowski declares himself a teacher—but not a teacher of many, a teacher of Performer. He emphasizes that the singular is important. He is speaking in this text about rare cases of apprenticeship. The text begins with two important definitions:

1   **Performer** (with a capital P) is a man of action; a state of being; a man of knowledge; a rebel who should conquer knowledge; an outsider; a warrior; a *pontifex*, a bridge-maker; a bridge between the witness and something else.

2   **Ritual** is performance, an accomplished action, an act. Plays, shows, spectacles are degenerated ritual; ritual is a time of great intensity; provoked intensity; when life becomes rhythm.

Ritual is a word that has haunted Grotowski since his early days in the theatre. In his theatre productions, he was often accused of trying to fashion new rituals for the audience. During paratheatre, critics attacked him for trying to create a public ritual and, in Theatre of Sources, for appropriating the rituals of traditional cultures. In his final phase of research, Ritual Arts or Art as Vehicle, he finds the way to articulate, in words and practice, his relation with ritual: ritual is action and Performer is the doer. He now attempts to create a ritual for the doer—to lead a rare person toward his/her **essence**.

Essence, for Grotowski, has nothing to do with learned social behavior or personality. Essence is "what you did not receive from others, what did not come from outside, what is not learned" (Grotowski 1988: 377). In order to identify essence better, Grotowski makes the distinction between feeling guilty for breaking society's moral code and feeling remorse for acting against your conscience. The feeling of remorse is linked to your essence—"this is between you and yourself, not between you and society" (Grotowski 1988: 377). How does one connect with one's essence? In certain young warriors at the peak of their organicity, the essence and the body merge as one. But this is a temporary state, associated with the vitality of youth. Grotowski is more interested in how to pass from the **body-and-essence** to the **body of essence**. He proposes this task of "personal transmutation" as a necessary challenge that each of us faces and he poses to us a key question: What is your process?

At this point, Grotowski's source-seeking arrives to a very old idea—that of Plato's Myth of Er. Psychologist James Hillman, in his book *The Soul's Code*, succinctly describes Plato's story:

> The soul of each of us is given a unique daimon before we are born, and it has selected an image or pattern that we live on earth. This soul-companion, the daimon, guides us here; in the process of arrival, however, we forget all that took place and believe we come empty into this world. The daimon remembers what is in your image and belongs to your pattern, and therefore your daimon is the carrier of your destiny.
>
> (Hillman 1996: 8)

We each have a destiny or process, and it is our mission to discover what it is. This concept has many names and has appeared throughout the centuries in diverse cultures. Hillman laments that this ancient aspect of psychology is usually relegated to the backburners of the paranormal, magic, religion, or the occult. Grotowski, too, recognized the mumbo-jumbo dangers of his research. But both Hillman and Grotowski determine that the concept of essence and process or soul and destiny is at the core of a human being's healthy existence and must be readmitted into contemporary thought.

Grotowski's way to rescue "the inner man" (another term for essence) is through performing— "With Performer, performing can become near process..." (Grotowski 1988: 377)—and through the relation of teacher and apprentice. He describes Performer's journey toward the body of essence and the need for precision and rigor, for mastery and simplicity, and for the teacher's reflective gaze. Once Performer has traced what Grotowski calls "the junction I-I," the teacher can withdraw. This I-I is a silent presence. We are reminded once more of the secure partner. It is not a separate or judging look. To develop the I-I is to work the process.

Grotowski also speaks of memory as a possible departure point in working one's process:

> One access to the creative way consists of discovering in yourself an ancient corporality to which you are bound by a strong ancestral relation. So you are neither in the character nor in the non-character. Starting from details you can discover in you somebody other—your grandfather, your mother.
>
> (Grotowski 1988: 379)

Grotowski eventually traces this search for an ancient corporality back to Performer of the primal ritual—to the beginning. He wonders: "Is essence the hidden background of memory?" (Grotowski 1988: 379). He has journeyed from body-memory to body-life to the body-and-essence to arrive to the body of essence and back to the actualization of memory. Grotowski claims a breakthrough, a rediscovery. But to what exactly has he found the key? When memory actualizes, "strong potentialities are activated." Is it the key to creativity?

Grotowski ends "Performer" with the citation from Meister Eckhart about breakthrough discussed earlier. Breakthrough, in German *Durchbruch*, is a word supposedly invented by the mystic Eckhart himself. The montage Grotowski has fashioned describes poetically a process of energy transformation and connects to Eckhart's creation spirituality which privileges the artist in us and among us: "in this breakthrough I discover that I and God are one" (Eckhart 1991: 302). It is interesting to note that Grotowski uses the words of a Western medieval mystic to conclude "Performer," one of his most personal and esoteric texts. He does not resort to Indian or Asian sources, but puts his work in line with a very European tradition that is connected to what he refers to as the "Mediterranean cradle." With "Performer," Grotowski himself returns to his sources.

SUMMARY

Now that we have reviewed Grotowski's key writings we can see plainly how the four notions of sacrifice, presence, totality, and the literalness of action have evolved throughout his work and thoughts. Sacrifice appears in the early theatre production work as *via negativa*, in parateatre as disarmament, and in later phases of his research as untaming. The aspect of sacrifice also resounds in the harsh work ethic and demands made by Grotowski on those selected to accompany him on his search. Grotowski's preoccupation with presence (the here and now) can be demonstrated by the work devoted to attention, awareness, perception, vigilance, and the privileging of body techniques over more psychological or mental methodologies. Totality is the aim—a fusion of the mind and body—and a connection to the essence, that which precedes any social conditioning. And, finally, for action to be true, it must be literal. The performer should seek a way to do her doings without pretence. Then she is present, total, and making the supreme sacrifice of revelation, of truth and honesty in what she is doing—she is organic. By keeping these four concepts in the forefront, we can now turn to a discussion of Grotowski as director and three distinct performative events from his body of work.

3

GROTOWSKI AS DIRECTOR

Grotowski ranks with Stanislavsky, Meyerhold, and Brecht as one of the four great stage directors of the twentieth century. But while it is generally understood that Stanislavsky transformed acting, Meyerhold, directing, and Brecht, playwrighting, Grotowski's influence on the craft is not so instantly recognizable. A more detailed analysis of Grotowski's work as a director will clarify his key contributions to the field of theatre.

GROTOWSKI IN REHEARSAL

During Theatre of Productions, Grotowski always dealt with established scripts. Even his final theatre production, *Apocalypsis cum figuris*, began rehearsals as a version of a conventional play. He stated time and again that he had no method, but approached each play in a different manner. Nor did he direct a play in order to make a point or teach a lesson. Grotowski directed plays to look for the unknown and to seek answers to his personal questions—and the questions usually involved looking for the meaning in human existence. Although he had no recipe for directing, one can formulate some basic principles concerning **archetypes**, **scenic equivalents**, **improvisation**, and **montage** from Grotowski's theatre work.

ARCHETYPES

During the early period of Theatre of Productions, Grotowski first would try to identify and confront the archetype in each text he directed. Recall that archetype, for Grotowski, is the myth itself and refers to the basic human situation in the text. Barba gives several examples of archetypes:

> Prometheus and the Sacrificial Lamb correspond to the archetype of the individual sacrificed for the community. Faustus and Einstein (in the imagination of the masses) correspond to the archetype of the Shaman who has surrendered to the Devil and in exchange has received a special knowledge of the universe.
>
> (Barba 1965: 74)

In *Kordian*, Grotowski worked with the archetype of the hero who tries to save the world by himself. In *Akropolis*, the archetype is what the playwright Wyspianski refers to as the "cemetery of the tribes," the place where Western civilization reaches its summit.

SCENIC EQUIVALENTS

After identifying the archetype in a text, Grotowski and his actors constructed what Barba calls "scenic equivalents" (Barba 1999: 39). These scenic equivalents (also sometimes called *etudes*, sketches, or propositions) were often developed directly from the text. But the actors never merely illustrated the scene from the play. In collaboration with Grotowski, they freely altered the form in a variety of ways.

For example, *Kordian* is a play about a young nineteenth-century Pole who wants to free his country from Russian rule. He tries to assassinate the czar, is committed to an asylum, eventually declared sane, and executed. When analyzing the play, Grotowski decided that any person who tries to save the world by himself in today's society is either insane or a child. He saw the asylum as the key to the play and so he set his production in a mental hospital. The various scenes and characters in the play took on the form of a madman's hallucinations. In Słowacki's play, Kordian delivers a patriotic speech on a mountain offering to sacrifice himself for Poland. Grotowski's Kordian delivered this soliloquy while an evil doctor drew blood from his arm.

The scenic equivalents served two purposes. First, as he attempts to incarnate the myth, the actor can connect to the "roots" of the myth and perceive those roots while taking into account his own experience. If this happens, then something in the life-mask of the actor splits and falls away, revealing a deeper, more intimate and human layer. This revelation, a kind of confession, came to be called the **total act**. (See Chapter 1.)

Second, in this act of exposing herself, the actor reveals herself as a human being: "even with the loss of a 'common sky' of belief and the loss of impregnable boundaries, the perceptivity of the human being remains" (Grotowski 2002: 23). In this moment, the actor returns "to a concrete mythical situation, to an experience of common human truth" (Grotowski 2002: 23). When this happens, performance, for Grotowski, becomes an **act of transgression**:

> Why are we concerned with art? To cross our frontiers, exceed our limitations, fill our emptiness—fulfill ourselves. This is not a condition but a process in which what is dark in us slowly becomes transparent. In this struggle with one's own truth, this effort to peel off the life-mask, the theatre, with its full-fleshed perceptivity, has always seemed to me a place of provocation. It is capable of challenging itself and its audience by violating accepted stereotypes of vision, feeling, and judgment—more jarring because it is imaged in the human organism's breath, body, and inner impulses. This defiance of taboo, this transgression, provides the shock which rips off the mask, enabling us to give ourselves nakedly to something which is impossible to define but which contains Eros and Caritas.
>
> (Grotowski 2002: 21–2)

GROTOWSKI AND IMPROVISATION

How did the scenic equivalents come into being? In his book *Theatre Trip*, Michael Smith describes what he observed at several rehearsals in Wroclaw in the late 1960s. Grotowski felt that Smith's version of events conveyed accurately one aspect of the rehearsal process at the Laboratory Theatre. He underlined, however, that there were other rehearsals which were never open to observation and that those rehearsals took on other dimensions.

Michael Smith was invited to attend an early rehearsal of what eventually became *Apocalypsis cum figuris*. He describes the church-like atmosphere, the silence, and whispered tones. Grotowski in dark glasses, sitting at a small desk in the corner, began the rehearsal by reading a selection by Dostoevsky about witches to the twelve actors. The actors were then sent to prepare themselves and returned sometime later in costume to begin the improvisation.

We use the term "improvisation" reluctantly. Grotowski rejected this term in relation to his work because of its association with an undisciplined and chaotic way of working. He often searched for another word to replace improvisation. (In later years, the word "rendering" was proposed, but Grotowski himself never accepted this word. **Rendering** has, however, become an important term in New World Performance Laboratory's work process.) Improvisation, in Grotowski's theatre, was an extremely rigorous activity that demanded the actor and the director to engage creatively in a personal confrontation with the core material.

As the improvisation proceeded, Grotowski sometimes called "Stop!" and the actors would freeze while he whispered or shouted new instructions or stimulated them physically. Other times he would enter the action without interrupting and physically move the actors in the space. The actors never cut their flow, stopped to ask questions, or surrendered to confusion. They uttered no words. Instead, they hummed, sang, and vocalized with gibberish or abstract sounds. Sometimes Grotowski would join the cacophony, singing or laughing, and wave his arms to encourage them further. He also might stop everything and have an actor repeat an action.

After the long, complicated improvisation, the actors wrote down everything they could remember about what they had done (Figure 3.1). They would divide the pages in their notebooks into two columns: one for actions and one for associations. This took about 30 minutes. Then they began a discussion amongst themselves in which they each talked about the improvisation. Grotowski mostly listened and watched. The next day began the work of reconstruction.

The majority of work in rehearsals consisted of "reconstructing" improvisations. Once the first improvisation was accomplished, the actors were responsible for remembering it in complete detail. Small bits of the improvisation might be isolated and worked and then put back into the whole. Other fragments might eventually be cut or the order of the events changed.

Material for the performance is slowly gathered. In league with the director, the essential points are identified and repeated many times. Everything that is not essential is eliminated. The exterior response is

Figure 3.1 Ludwik Flaszen, Zbigniew Cynkutis, Antoni Jahołkowski, Rena Mirecka, Jerzy Grotowski, Ryszard Cieślak, Maja Komorowska, and Stanisław Scierski in Paris (1966). Photograph by Andrzej Paluchiewicz

scored and fixed as the sign. The impulse flows through the sign. In this way, the montage is created and the actors' score is built from the flow of living impulses.

GROTOWSKI AND MONTAGE

Grotowski usually made an initial adaptation of the script before rehearsals began. He called this reworking of the script a textual **montage**. Most of the time, roles were cast and even the spatial relationship for the production already decided. Grotowski often reprimanded young directors who try to develop a theatre piece without the structure provided by a script. He pointed out that it was only his final production that might be considered a collective creation, starting from zero, and he stressed how much one learns as a director and actor from working within the limits set by the great dramatic texts.

When he worked with a script, Grotowski structured the textual montage so that a meeting could take place, a confrontation. He did not seek to illustrate the text or even identify with it. He eliminated anything that was not important for him and selected those words that could function with regard to his own experience or that of the actors. He might change the order of scenes or rearrange sentences, but he seldom added text from other sources. In *Akropolis*, though, he did add some text from the playwright Wyspianski's letters and also from a review of the dramatic text. Ludwik Flaszen, writing in his initial notes about the production, said that "Of all the plays Grotowski directed, *Akropolis* is the least faithful to its literary original" (Grotowski 2002: 61). However, in a personal conversation almost 30 years later, Flaszen stated that he felt *Akropolis* was a masterpiece in editing and in its faithfulness to the spirit of the original.

During rehearsals, the montage would continue to change and take on its new form. However, no matter how many changes Grotowski might make in a text, he felt he treated the playwright's work with respect and retained "the inner meaning of the play" (Flaszen in Grotowski 2002: 99). Eric Bentley takes umbrage with this presumption:

> In your notes on *The Constant Prince* you congratulate yourself on catching "the inner meaning of the play." Cool it. The inner meaning of a three-act masterpiece cannot be translated into any one-act dance drama. Its meaning is tied indissolubly to its three-act structure: otherwise Calderon himself would have reduced it to one act—he was a master of the one act.
>
> (Bentley 1969: 169)

Bentley makes his point. He goes on to say that what Grotowski has accomplished with his montage is another play, his own, not Calderon's.

Grotowski refashioned dramatic texts to fit his own "here and now." The works (especially *Akropolis*, *Dr. Faustus*, and *The Constant Prince*) became organic frameworks for a particular group of actors living in Poland at a particular moment in the country's history to confront questions from their own lives. This is not new in the theatre. Even Shakespeare did it all the time.

> The principle is the following—it is very clear if you understand the creative situation of the actor—one asks the actors who play Hamlet to recreate their own Hamlet. That is, do the same thing that Shakespeare did with the

traditional Hamlet [. . .] Every great creator builds bridges between the past and himself, between his roots and his being. That is the only sense in which the artist is a priest: pontifex in Latin, he who builds bridges [. . .]. It's the same with the creativity of the actor. He must not illustrate Hamlet, he must meet Hamlet. The actor must give his cue within the context of his own experience. And the same for the director. I didn't do Wyspianski's *Akropolis*, I met it. I didn't think or analyze Auschwitz from the outside; it's this thing in me which is something I didn't know directly, but indirectly I knew very well.

(Grotowski cited in Schneider and Cody 2001: 245)

What Grotowski describes here is one aspect of what some critics called **the dialectic of apotheosis and derision**, an abiding principle throughout the Theatre of Production phase of his work. It was also referred to as "collision with the roots" or "religion expressed through blasphemy; love speaking out through hate" (Grotowski cited in Schechner and Wolford 2001: 22). Raised on the works of **Marx** and **Hegel** and strongly influenced by his personal fascination for Asian philosophy, Grotowski naturally leaned toward a dialectic structure in his work. This means that he often examined ideas by trying to reconcile the opposites of the argument. In the company's practice, this principle came to be called the *conjunctio-oppositorum* and this **conjunction of opposites** eventually found its way into all aspects of the company's training and production work.

> **Georg Wilhelm Friedrich Hegel (1770–1831)**: German philosopher, perhaps best known for his concept of dialectic, which can be summarized in three phases: thesis (e.g. the French Revolution); antithesis (the reign of terror which followed); and synthesis (a constitutional democracy).

> **Karl Marx (1818–83)**: German philosopher and political economist whose writings, especially *The Communist Manifesto* (1847–8), influenced much of the twentieth century's politics, philosophy, and economic theory.

Conjunctio-oppositorum

Conjunctio-oppositorum is a term used by Grotowski to illustrate the basic dialectic between rigor and life in the work of an actor. On one hand, Grotowski was always looking for very spontaneous impulses to free the way toward the interior core from where great acting arises (*hic et nunc*), while at the same time, demanding the most precise structure possible.

When dealing with the mystery of "time" in theatre, actors encounter the difficulty of being in the present moment, in the transitory "now." Actors find themselves in the dilemma of trying to escape from the nagging question: "What next?" In order to free oneself from this pesky question, Grotowski always demanded a very clear structure or score of actions from the actor. Precision and organicity form the two opposing poles of Grotowski's paradoxical conjunction.

Grotowski was always pointing out the precision in the "artificial." He used the word artificial in its most positive sense, meaning a structure of formal details and signs. Then he would contrast this structure (artificiality) with the organicity of the impulses from which these details or signs emerged. At different moments in his creative life, Grotowski revisited this dialectic. He found it in the basic conjunction of the word *hatha* (in hatha yoga)—where the energy of the Moon (*ha*) and the energy of the Sun (*tha*) are in complete balance. He also found this conjunction of opposites in observing the artificial process of the actors of the Peking Opera where the organic process is integrated through very small pauses in the centuries old scores of the different characters. On the other hand, he observed the phenomenon as well in the ceremonies of the Voodoo tradition where the apparent spontaneity of the "possessed" is supported by a very clear and long-established ritual structure and by the lucid doings of each *loa* (or spirit) from the Afro-Caribbean pantheon. The dialectic between rigor and life is at the core of the principle of *conjunctio-oppositorum* and permeates all of Grotowski's work as a director—both in and out of the theatre.

OTHER ASPECTS OF MONTAGE

Montage does not only concern the editing work on the text, however. It also functions in another way in Grotowski's work. The term montage can be traced to Russian film director **Sergei Eisenstein (1898–1948)**. For Eisenstein, montage refers to the flow of assembled images that create an understandable whole. These images may move rapidly and even seem disconnected, but when viewed together in sequence, they lead the spectator to comprehend a story or theme. Montage, used in this sense, remained an important concept for Grotowski through the final period of his work, Art as Vehicle or Ritual Arts.

In his article "From the Theatre Company to Art as Vehicle," Grotowski discusses the **seat of the montage**, and makes the distinction between the seat of the montage in the perception of the spectator and in the doer (Grotowski 1993: 124). To make his point, he gives the example of *The Constant Prince* where Ryszard Cieślak, in the leading role, developed a score of action based on a sensual memory, an erotic experience, from his early youth.

> The moment of which I speak was, therefore, immune from every dark connotation, it was as if this remembered adolescent liberated himself with his body from the body itself, as if he liberated himself—step after step— from the heaviness of the body, from any painful aspect. And, on the river of the memory, of its most minute impulses and actions, he put the monologues of the Constant Prince.
>
> (Grotowski 1993: 123)

However, while Cieślak was engaged in remembering his "carnal prayer," everything around him, the *mise en scene*, was organized to make the spectator comprehend the story of a martyr suffering unspeakable tortures for his beliefs. The content of Calderon/Słowacki's play, the structure and logic of the written text, the narrative elements around and in relation to what Cieślak was doing (especially the actions of the other actors), all suggested to the spectator that the story of a martyr was being played out in front of them. The story of the play appeared in the perception of the spectator. The actors were doing something else. Essentially, Grotowski was directing two ensembles.

> To make the montage in the spectator's perception is the task of the director, and it is one of the most important elements of his craft. As director of *The Constant Prince*, I worked with premeditation to create this type of montage, and so that the majority of the spectators captured the same montage: the story of a martyr, of a prisoner surrounded by his persecutors, who look to crush him, but in the same time are fascinated by him, etc...All this was

conceived in a quasi-mathematical way, so that this montage functioned and was accomplishing itself in the perception of the spectator.

(Grotowski 1995: 124)

THE PRINCIPLE OF NO-CHARACTER

Grotowski believed that human beings play so many roles in their daily lives that the theatre should be the place where the actor does not play a character, but tries to seek a more authentic self. This principle was revolutionary. In working with the actors of the Laboratory Theatre, Grotowski often directed them not to play "characters." Each performance became a challenge for the actors to strip off their own masks, to uncover themselves, and demonstrate the truth. They were able to do this behind the protection of the *mise en scene*. They were playing themselves, but through the *mise en scene*, the audience understood them as characters. The audience understood one thing, but the actors were actually doing something else. Perhaps it will be easier to understand this principle by describing Grotowski's work with Ryszard Cieślak in *The Constant Prince*.

GROTOWSKI AND THE ACTOR

Grotowski's role in giving birth to Cieślak's performance in *The Constant Prince* (Figure 3.2) cannot be underestimated. When Cieślak first arrived to work with the group he was full of blocks—psychologically, physically, and vocally. Cieślak's liberation was only possible because it was accomplished in tandem with Grotowski himself. It might even be said that the two of them—actor and director—liberated each other. In a 1975 interview, Grotowski spoke frankly, yet obliquely, about this period of his life. He framed it as a transition from someone who depended on domination to prove his existence to someone capable of opening himself to another human being.

JG: Most likely the central problem of my non-existence was that I felt a lack of relationship with others, because any relationship I had was not completely real. And the more domination there was on my side, the more it had to be unreal.

AB: You were afraid of people?

JG: Yes.

AB: You were afraid of people, you didn't love them or yourself?

Figure 3.2 Ryszard Cieślak in *The Constant Prince* (1965). Photographer unknown, courtesy of the Archive of the Grotowski Centre, Wroclaw

JG: I loved them so much it sometimes seemed to me that I would
      die—from despair. Then again I didn't love them and was afraid.
      Occasionally, there was aggression: since you don't love me, I will
      hate you. I want to stress that this trismus had already passed away
      before the satiation with public opinion and prestige. I have heard it
      said that prestige subdued me, and that's an attractive alternative,
      but it's not the case. Human relations brought about the change. What
      appeared to be an interest in the art of acting proved to be a search
      for and discovery of partnership (and the trismus faded when I was
      able to grasp this)—with Someone, someone else—and someone
      who, in the moment of action, at the time of work, I defined then in
      words used to define God. At that time this meant, for me—the son of
      man. Everything was transformed, became dramatic and painful, and
      there was still something of a predatory nature. But it was already
      something very different. And then there was a fading away.

(Grotowski 1975: 219–20)

Grotowski's honesty here is striking. In the work accomplished with
Cieślak, he reached a remarkable point, a kind of symbiosis with another
human being. The "leading motif" he spoke of previously—the question
"who-am-I?" and the problems of human loneliness and the inevitability
of death—are put into practice, are made flesh, in the director–actor
relationship forged with Cieślak. Grotowski said their connection went
"beyond all the limits of the technique, of a philosophy, or of ordinary
habits" (cited in Richards 1995: 16).

People have remarked that it was difficult to speak about one without the other. The being performing was more like Cieślak–Grotowski,
not just Cieślak. Grotowski himself said it was not like two human
beings working, but a double human being (cited in Richards 1995: 16).
We believe that the essence of Grotowski's theatre does not lie in the
actor–spectator relationship as many suppose nor in his dramaturgy or
mise en scene, but in the relationship between the actor and the director
that reached its first fruition in the work on *The Constant Prince*. In the
safety and privacy of rehearsal, Grotowski realized that a real meeting
can take place between two people and it was this discovery that formed
the basis for all of his future work inside and outside the theatre.

During the preparation of *The Constant Prince*, Grotowski and Cieślak
worked for many months together alone, without the rest of the company,
meticulously constructing the physical score, Cieślak's "re-membering" of

his adolescent ecstasy. The text was worked separately. First, Cieślak memorized it precisely to the point that he could begin at any spot without a mistake. Grotowski would appear at Cieślak's bedside in the middle of the night, wake him up, and make him recite the text word for word. Once the text was well memorized, it was placed in relation to the physical score. Once the physical score was clearly delineated, it was placed in relation to the work of the other actors. The result of this unique creative process was a performance lauded throughout the world and the heralding of a new acting method. But any attempts to imitate Grotowski–Cieślak's creation failed miserably. To copy the externals of the performance and ignore the essential aspect of the phenomenon, the actor–director relationship, often led to grotesque interpretations of the new so-called Grotowski method and missed the underlying principle at play in the work.

> There is something incomparably intimate and productive in the work with the actor entrusted to me. He must be attentive and confident and free, for our labor is to explore his possibilities to the utmost. His growth is attended by observation, astonishment, and desire to help; my growth is projected onto him, or, rather, is *found in him*—and our common growth becomes revelation. This is not instruction of a pupil but utter opening to another person, in which the phenomenon of "shared or double birth" becomes possible. The actor is reborn—not only as an actor but as a man—and with him, I am reborn. It is a clumsy way of expressing it, but what is achieved is a total acceptance of one human being by another.
>
> (Grotowski 2002: 25)

What Grotowski describes here is a kind of sublimation of the self. Often, this aspect of egolessness gets missed in discussing Grotowski's theatre. Some scholars, such as Timothy Wiles (1980), have criticized Grotowski's *via negativa* by asking, "What does the actor do when all the blocks have been eliminated?" Grotowski laughed after reading one such article. "To be empty is exactly the point," he said. How does one become liberated from the ego? By arriving to the point of emptiness, the Void. Barba makes the connection with this crucial aspect of Grotowski's work and the Hindu doctrine of *Sunyata*:

> *Sunyata*, the Void, is not nothingness. It is non-duality in which the object does not differ from the subject. The self and belief in the self are the causes of error and pain. The way to escape from error and pain is to eliminate the self.

> This is the Perfect Wisdom, the enlightenment that can be attained through
> a *via negativa*, denying worldly categories and phenomenons to the point of
> denying the self and, by so doing, reaching the Void.
>
> (Barba 1999: 49)

One of the best descriptions of Cieślak's performance is by Stefan
Brecht writing, brilliantly yet often critically, after the Laboratory Theatre's
New York tour in 1969. He clearly depicts Cieślak as an illustration of the
via negativa, as an empty vessel through which "emotional and volitional
states of the spirit" are expressed. "The Grotowskian actor actualizes spirit
for us by diffusing his ego through his body. However shitty its nuance,
this approach is a theatrical revolution. It opposes ego-theatre" (Brecht
1970: 128). This "no-ego theatre" seems even more revolutionary today
than it did 40 years ago. As young actors on the fast track to Broadway or
Hollywood revel in the cult of personality that show business engenders,
today's theatre moves farther and farther from its spiritual foundations.
Grotowski, however, offers another possibility. He assumes that the boundaries of the ego can be transcended (or dissolved) and he accomplished it,
for the first time, in his work with Ryszard Cieślak.

RYSZARD CIEŚLAK

Many consider Cieślak the best actor of his generation. Anyone who
witnessed his performance in *The Constant Prince* never forgot it. He
played a major role in Grotowski's final production and acknowledged
masterpiece, *Apocalypsis cum figuris*, and was an important collaborator
in the paratheatre period of research. After the dissolution of the
Laboratory Theatre in 1984, Cieślak conducted workshops and directed
productions with various groups around the world. But he never again
reached the heights of his work on *The Constant Prince*. However, in the
1980s when he appeared on stage and on film as Dhritarastra, the blind
king, in Peter Brook's epic production of *The Mahabarata*, Cieślak
demonstrated his skill like an aging samurai who never forgets the
nuances of battle. Years later, in 1990, speaking at the "Homage to
Ryszard Cieślak" in Paris, after his death from lung cancer, Grotowski
referred again to what they accomplished together:

> We can say that I demanded from him everything, a courage in a certain
> way inhuman, but I never asked him to produce an effect. He needed five
> months more? Okay. Ten months more? Okay. Fifteen months more? Okay.

We just worked slowly. And after this symbiosis, he had a kind of total security in the work, he had no fear, and we saw that everything was possible because there was no fear.

(cited in Richards 1995: 16)

Everything was possible. In retrospect, one wonders about the power dynamics between Grotowski and Cieślak and the repercussions of their intimacy on the rest of the ensemble. Certainly jealousies flared and petty differences arose, but it was always left out of the workspace. Grotowski knew how to deflate potentially explosive situations and the actors trusted him implicitly. Grotowski never ascribed to the romantic concept of "group," so often associated with the 1960s and 1970s experimental theatre. He preferred the word "team" (Figure 3.3) where each member knew his/her job and could perform it impeccably. He made his team believe that everything was possible and from this brink of possibility, Grotowski led his actors to the highest heights of their craft and eventually beyond the boundaries of theatre.

Figure 3.3 Ryszard Cieślak and Rena Mirecka in the third version of *Apocalypsis cum figuris*, on the floor: Zbigniew Cynkutis (1973). Photograph by Piotr Baracz

ANALYSIS OF A KEY PRODUCTION: *AKROPOLIS*

As an example of Grotowski's work as a director of theatre productions, we have selected *Akropolis*. When Grotowski began work on *Akropolis* in 1962 he knew he needed a "hit." The production was constructed, more than the previous works of the Laboratory Theatre, to illustrate the work being done in Opole and to garner international attention. It worked. *Akropolis* was performed to acclaim throughout the world for approximately eight years. It is arguably the production most commonly associated with Grotowski and his theatre and is the only production readily available on video. Grotowski actually had a hand in editing the video document and it demonstrates clearly many of the principles of the Theatre of Productions period of his work. Furthermore, the renowned **Wooster Group** revisited Grotowski's production of *Akropolis* in recent years in a performance entitled *Poor Theatre*, a simulacrum and homage to the technical mastery and emotional impact of the Polish Laboratory Theatre's accomplishment as well as a testament to its continuing importance in the history of theatre.

Wooster Group: New York based avant-garde theatre company, under the direction of Elizabeth Lecompte (b. 1944). Operating since 1975, founding members include Willem Dafoe (b. 1955) and Spalding Gray (1941–2004).

GROTOWSKI AND THE PLAY

Akropolis by Stanisław Wyspiański is a classic Polish play, first published in 1904 and first performed in 1926. Its style and form fit securely into the Polish Romantic tradition as a highly poetic, religious, and political statement to the Polish nation. In the cathedral in Krakow, where many of Poland's kings, poets, and heroes lie buried, hangs a series of tapestries from the sixteenth century depicting scenes from ancient mythology and the Bible. The play turns around the folk belief that on the eve of Christ's Resurrection, the characters from these tapestries come to life. Wyspiański hoped to depict the sum total of Western civilization's contributions to humanity and juxtapose that with the Polish experience. He called the Polish cathedral the cemetery of the tribes, "our Acropolis," and his characters reenact key moments from the Mediterranean cradle's cultural history, heroically celebrating human accomplishment. For Wyspianski, "Acropolis" is the symbol of any civilization's highest achievement.

Grotowski, in deciding to mount *Akropolis*, asked himself one question: What is the cemetery of the tribes for us today in Poland in 1962? What is our Acropolis, the symbol of our generation's highest achievement? Applying his dialectic of apotheosis and derision, Grotowski cruelly and ironically places the poet's drama in the twentieth century's most horrible invention: the concentration camp—a place where human values reached both their lowest and highest point.

Another source of inspiration for the production was the words of Polish poet Tadeusz Borowski, a survivor of the Auschwitz concentration camp:

It's just scrap iron that will be left after us
And a hollow, derisive laugher of future generations.

(cited in Kumiega 1985: 60)

Armed with this framework, and with the collaboration of prominent Polish designer and Auschwitz survivor, **Josef Szajna (b. 1922)**, Grotowski set out to bring to life onstage the brutal truth of the concentration camp.

In the video presentation of *Akropolis*, Peter Brook refers to the international contest that was held to find a work of art that might symbolize the tragedy of the concentration camps. It was finally decided that nothing could do justice to the camp's horror except the camp itself. So the authorities left the concentration camp at Auschwitz intact as a reminder for future generations of a terrible moment in humanity's history. Brook then discusses the problems of staging the concentration camp's terror. He mentions Peter Weiss's play *The Investigation* which takes a documentary approach in dealing with the events. But Grotowski and his actors found another way. Brook states that Grotowski's production actualized once more the essence of the concentration camp in space and time in the theatre. Grotowski was very careful to approach the material without any kind of sentimentality. It was to be a merciless depiction and the prisoners would not be glorified or descend into emotional soup. But how could they accomplish this?

THE SPACE

In conceiving the actor–spectator relationship, it was decided that there would be no direct participation from the audience. Grotowski cast the two ensembles, actors and spectators, in two precise roles: the actors became the dead and the spectators the living. The actors, as the resurrected inmates of the concentration camp, carry out their actions in such close proximity to the spectators that their presence gives "the impression that they are born from a dream of the living" (Flaszen 1965: 63). The dead perform for the living and the spectators witness (or dream) humanity's nightmare.

The space designed for *Akropolis* consists of a huge box in the middle of the room with a variety of metal junk piled on top of it (Figure 3.4). Stovepipes of various sizes, two old wheelbarrows, a bathtub, hammers and nails will be used by the actors to build their own crematorium. They hang these rusty elements from wires or pound them into the floor throughout the hour-long performance. These highly rhythmic moments of building activity are interspersed with periods of "daydreaming," in which the inmates reenact their own versions of the biblical stories and myths from Wyspiański's play. Grotowski touches here the phenomenon of prisoners

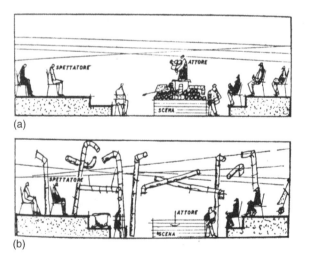

(a)

(b)

Figure 3.4 A plan of the space for *Akropolis*, 1962. Design: Jerzy Gurawski
    (a) The room at the beginning of the performance
    (b) The room at the end of the performance

who fashion their own reality when under the pressures of violence and incarceration. The prisoners are their own torturers, betraying each other, struggling for a moment of respite or beauty, as they build this fantastic and cruel community—a community that becomes more real than any theatrical illusion of the real thing itself could ever hope to be.

Grotowski created *Akropolis* with his actors in Opole, only 60 miles from Auschwitz, one of the Nazi's most notorious extermination camps. The nearness of the camp exerted a heavy influence on the company's work. Grotowski fought against any kind of theatrical compromise of the material. In a 1968 interview he said: "We did not wish to have a stereo-typed production with evil SS men and noble prisoners. We cannot play prisoners, we cannot create such images in the theatre. Any documentary film is stronger. We looked for something else . . . No realistic illusions, no prisoners' costumes" (cited in Kumiega 1985: 63).

THE COSTUMES AND PROPS

Josef Szajna designed the costumes and properties for the production, while Grotowski's customary collaborator, Jerzy Gurawski supervised the scenic architecture. The costumes consisted of old burlap potato sacks. The sacks were cut full of holes and then lined with fabric to suggest torn flesh. The actors wore heavy wooden soled shoes and dark berets. Eugenio Barba, who served as assistant director for *Akropolis*, describes watching Szajna cut up the burlap and sew each garment by hand "with his shirt sleeves rolled up over his Auschwitz tattoo" (Barba 1999: 34). Szajna designed a poetic version of the concentration-camp uniform that erased all outward indications of gender, age, and social class. Anonymity reigned. The spectator saw only the tortured bodies of a community of the dead.

It is in his notes to *Akropolis* that Ludwik Flaszen first develops his definition of "poor theatre": "It is absolutely forbidden to introduce in the play anything which is not already there at the very beginning" (Flaszen 1965: 75). Given this rule, each object on stage finds various uses throughout the performance. For example, the very normal bathtub represents the tubs used in the concentration camps to boil human bodies to make soap and process leather. Turned upside down the same object becomes an altar where an inmate prays; in another moment it becomes the Biblical hero Jacob's wedding bed. The wheel-barrows are used for transporting corpses, but also become angelic wings in Jacob's fight with an angel or the Trojan king's throne in the story of Paris and Helen.

In one brilliantly grotesque moment, Jacob transforms a stovepipe into his bride, Rachel, and leads her in a joyous procession through the cramped space. This scene is particularly interesting because, in an early version, Rachel was played by actress Maja Komarowska. When she left the company, the stovepipe was substituted for her in this key moment in the play. This is a fine example of Grotowski's ability to turn a misfortune into a magic moment. In his rehearsal room, there were never problems only creative solutions.

In *Akropolis*, the actors fashion a myriad of worlds with a small number of ordinary objects. The result sometimes reminds one of children innocently playing. All of this produces a grotesque juxtaposition with the stark brutality of the concentration camp itself.

THE FACIAL MASK

During early rehearsals, Grotowski realized that some of the actors easily slipped into an emotional attitude when confronted with the concentration-camp material. He devised a special training for the group. In **Rainer Maria Rilke's** essay about the sculptor Rodin, he describes the artist's ability to read a person's past and future from the wrinkles on his face. Grotowski took this suggestion literally and began to ask the actors to recreate facial masks based on photographs of actual concentration-camp inmates. Grotowski guided the actors to select and freeze sneers, scowls, frowns, and other expressions. He sought expressions that connected as well to each actor's own personality and typical reactions.

Rainer Maria Rilke (1875–1926): Often considered Germany's greatest twentieth-century poet. His collections include: *Duino Elegies* (1912/1922) and *Sonnets to Orpheus* (1922).

Grotowski understood that the human mask is often formed by one's habitual thoughts and intentions in life. If someone is constantly repeating, "Everyone's against me!" or "I'll never get anywhere!" these phrases leave traces on our bodies and faces. He asked each actor to choose a "slogan," a personally appropriate phrase that could be repeated silently over and over. In this way, each actor's mask was slowly constructed, without the use of makeup or prosthetics, only by mastery of facial muscles, the repetition of a slogan, and a truthful response to the director's proposals.

The actor's face stayed frozen in this mask throughout the performance, providing a strong emotional impact which transcended the obvious artificiality of the effect. The mask, with lifeless eyes that looked beyond the spectator, jarringly duplicated the single expression (or expressionlessness) apparent in the photographs during the last stage of survival prior to extermination. But each mask also was unique to the individual actor and mysteriously revealed something essential about each of the actors, perhaps linked to their personal attitude and reactions face to the Holocaust material, Europe's history of anti-Semitism, and Wyspiański's nationalistic Polish drama.

Grotowski's work on the facial mask was used only during *Akropolis*. It was not a method that he applied, like a recipe, in other performances. In *Akropolis*, it served a clear purpose and proved to be a creative solution to a practical problem of craft.

THE ACTOR'S BODY: IS IT FORMALISM?

Eric Bently found Grotowski's *Akropolis* overly aesthetic and formal (Bentley 1969: 166). This was intentional. Grotowski was seeking a "non-emotive form of expression" (Flaszen cited in Kumiega 1985: 63). Another way he formalized the acting in *Akropolis* was through pantomime. The actors began to work with elements of classical pantomime and borrowed certain techniques to apply to the creation of their physical scores. This formed the beginning of the work on the famous *plastique* exercises (see Chapter 4). As you watch the actors working in the video, you can see them applying precise physical/movement principles. They often play with their equilibrium, throwing themselves off-balance or creating moments that are quasi-balletic in how they change weight, use gesture, and hold positions. Flaszen points out that each actor "has his own silhouette irrevocably fixed" (Flaszen 1965: 77).

The actors incorporate many stops into their scores—both as a group and individually. Zygmunt Molik recounts how Grotowski would often call out "Photo!" during rehearsals and the entire group would freeze, fixing the composition. These compositions were sometimes awkward statuesque poses, giving the impression of heroic monuments. The actors also apply "the Chinese principle," beginning a movement with a slight impulse in the opposite direction, and other aspects of opposition, creating tension by consciously engaging opposing vectors in their bodies and the relation with the space and each other. Years later at the Collège de France in Paris in 1997, Grotowski recalled: "[In *Akropolis*] everything was formal, but at the same time nothing was formal—everything was alive" (Grotowski 1997d, June 16, authors' translation).

THE SOUNDSCAPE

While the textual montage and physical composition of *Akropolis* are certainly remarkable, a contemporary witness is even more awed by the actors' vocal skills and the director's ingenious editing of a soundscape that accompanies each visual moment of the performance. The sound-scape includes singing, chanting, roars, purrs, and a myriad of inarticulate sounds uttered by the actors, as well as the rhythmic clomping of the wooden shoes, a melancholy violin, and the harsh metallic clang of hammers and nails. Each sound, spoken or otherwise, was precisely coordinated with the physical action. Flaszen explains how "The sounds are interwoven in a complex score which brings back fleetingly the memory of all the forms of language." He refers to the Tower of Babel effect, a "clash of foreign people and foreign languages meeting just before their extermination" (Flaszen 1965: 77). In *Akropolis*, voice becomes more than a means to communicate intellectually the meaning of words. It functions as "pure sound" and viscerally and emotionally affects the spectators even if they don't understand the Polish language.

Robert Findlay describes in detail how the actors brought to life Wyspiański's complex poetic text:

> Sometimes it was intentionally mumbled or occasionally spoken as if by children. At other times it was stated in a peasant dialect. There were litur-gical incantations as well as very sophisticated and melodious recitations. Most striking were those periods in which the performers used the artificial intonations of the traditional Nô actor.
>
> (Findlay 1984: 8)

Findlay goes on to state that the production was almost operatic because of the strong musical elements throughout the piece. This kind of musicality was a feature of all of Grotowski's production work. In fact, while the final stages of his research clearly were devoted to the investigation of song and vibration, this stream of inquiry was apparent from the early years of his work with actors. One could even say that all of Grotowski's performances were sung.

DESCRIPTION OF KEY SCENES FROM *AKROPOLIS*

THE PROLOGUE AND FIRST SCENES

Grotowski's *Akropolis* begins with Zygmunt Molik clomping into the space carrying a limp, headless dummy. Molik climbs to the top of the junk pile in the space, lays the dummy gently on the bathtub, and spews out a prologue that summarizes the action of the play. The words come from a letter by Wyspiański and a review of the play when it was first published. "I am reading scenes from *Akropolis*. I am pleased with them, and I have the impression that each scene has a breath of fresh air" (cited in Findlay 1984: 8). At this point, the other six actors (Ryszard Cieślak, Zbigniew Cynkutis, Rena Mirecka, Stanisław Scierski, Antoni Jahołkowski, and Andrzej Paluchiewicz) enter, marching, their wooden shoes mark the precise, rhythmic beat. They carry two wheelbarrows above their heads. Molik continues:

> Action: the night of Resurrection at Wawel cathedral, our Acropolis. It starts with the angels, who have come down to the floor, carrying the coffin of St. Stanislaw. Figures and statues from the cathedral tombstones coming alive. Jacob's dream, Jewish. Heroes of Troy, Helen and Paris, have come down from another tapestry [two male prisoners who will play Helen and Paris strike awkward, statuesque poses]. Conclusion: resurrected Christ the Saviour comes down to the floor from the main altar.
>
> (cited in Findlay 1984: 8–9)

Molik finishes his text in a quiet voice: "More fantastic and symbolic than any other play to date, this drama depicts the progress of the human race through its warlike and pastoral stages, with the power of song dominating throughout." He immediately places his violin under his chin and begins to play a strident, sentimental tune. The other prisoners snap to attention and start to assemble the pieces of stovepipe while chanting phrases from Wyspiański's play:

CHORUS:	On the cemetery of the tribes
	They come here for the day of sacrifice,
	On the cemetery of the tribes.
ONE VOICE:	Our Acropolis.
CHORUS:	Only once a year,
	They come only once a year
	On the cemetery of the tribes.
ONE VOICE:	Our Acropolis.
CHORUS:	They read the words of judgment
	On the cemetery of the tribes.
ONE VOICE:	Our Acropolis.
CHORUS:	They're gone and the smoke lingers on.

(cited in Findlay 1984: 9–10)

The focus shifts to two prisoners (Cieślak and Jahołkowski) carrying a stovepipe on their shoulders. In Wyspiański's text, they are angels. They walk in place, a stylized mime-type walk. They raise and lower the heavy load, and talk of the many corpses and interminable suffering. When they discover the headless dummy tossed aside, they realize there is one body still alive among the corpses: "Do you hear his groaning? Do you see his black face? Do you see his crown of thorns?" (cited in Findlay 1984: 10). When the body dies, the two prisoners hang the limp figure on one of the ropes stretched across the space—a shocking image of a prisoner gunned down while trying to climb the barbed wire—or is it Christ crucified? The violin plays and a second work period of rhythmic building and pounding begins.

The performance continues: short scenes of dialogue and striking imagery intermingled with the precisely orchestrated and choreographed work sequences. There is a scene where two prisoners are sorting the corpses' hair. They caress a large sheet of plastic and the scene transforms into Rena Mirecka performing a strange, puppetlike dance. There is a brutal scene of interrogation where two guards mechanically push a prisoner back and forth between them before hanging his exhausted body on the ropes and a grotesque scene where a female prisoner (Mirecka) forces another inmate to make love to her while she perches over him in the bathtub, laughing maniacally. After the sexual orgasm, she rejects him by violently pushing him back into the bathtub three times. Each of these scenes corresponds to a scene in Wyspiański's play.

THE STORY OF JACOB

Molik then announces that they will begin the "old Jewish story of Jacob," and he tells the basic plot points. Findlay says that "The Laboratorium's version of the biblical story followed generally the sequence of Wyspiański's text, but with considerable internal cutting and the elimination of Jacob's and Esau's final reconciliation" (Findlay 1984: 11–12).

One of the most memorable moments in this part of the performance is the marriage of Rachel and Jacob. Jacob and his uncle Laban have fought a tug-of-war over the worthless piece of plastic that represents Rachel. After Jacob kills his uncle, he takes possession of the plastic and sings a love song in which he calls her his bird of paradise. Another prisoner lying amidst the junk speaks Rachel's text: "Let's go to my father . . . I love only you" (cited in Findlay 1984: 13). Jacob drapes the piece of plastic on one of the stovepipes like a bridal veil. The prisoners form a procession behind Jacob and his stovepipe Rachel and sing a Polish wedding song. Mirecka rattles two nails to signify the ringing of the church bells as the procession winds its way toward the marriage bed, the bathtub.

The story continues with a long speech about Jacob's old age and his homesickness. He wrestles with an angel (Cynkutis) who lies in one of the wheelbarrows which Jacob takes on his back. Jacob asks: "Who are you who is stronger than all living men?" The angel replies: "Necessity" (cited in Findlay 1984: 13). After another frenzy of activity, the crematorium is completed and the prisoners, at a standstill, gaze upward, searching for the sun and moaning softly.

Jahołkowski suddenly interrupts this ghostly reverie. He moves from stovepipe to stovepipe, tapping each one with a nail, and speaking into the tubes to amplify his voice like a camp loudspeaker. He announces that a blackbird, a spy, has been captured. "The blackbird came to listen to our souls." He then proclaims: "The ice on the river is breaking. The first flowers are for Paris and Helen" (cited in Findlay 1984: 14). We are now transported to the landscape of Troy.

PARIS AND HELEN

During this part of the production, the actors put their arms inside their costumes. This simple transformation gives the impression of prisoners fighting the cold, while also suggesting the ruins of ancient Greek statues. Grotowski boldly casts a man to play the role of Helen. Scierski has played various women's roles throughout the piece, but in a simple love scene between Helen and Paris, where the other inmates, as guards, laugh and mock them, we are reminded that homosexuals, too, suffered in the Holocaust. When Paris tells Helen that it is time to go to bed, the others explode with vulgar hoots. This enactment of homosexual love was extremely bold for the time. At each moment in this production, Grotowski challenges his own culture's bigotry and reveals humanity's hypocrisy. Through constant repetition of the phrases, "our Acropolis," and "cemetery of the tribes," Grotowski and his actors reflect the evil and intolerance inherent in each person—inmate, guard, patriarch, matriarch, hero or goddess, as well as each spectator.

THE END OF THE PERFORMANCE

Wyspiański ends his drama with the resurrection of a Christ/Apollo figure. In typical Polish Romantic fashion, this messiah bears the nation's hopes toward the future. But in Grotowski's *Akropolis*, there is no hope (Figure 3.5). Molik, as King David, lists the accomplishments of his tribe. He raises his voice, crying, "When will God come?" and bursts into song. His voice vibrates through the space in a stupendous demonstration of the use of resonators. He sings using overtones—engaging both high and low resonators—like two different voices simultaneously. He raises the headless dummy above his head. Grotowski's Savior is an emaciated corpse from the concentration camps. The prisoners ecstatically sing Apollo's words from Wyspiański's text to the tune of a traditional Polish Christmas carol and begin a torturous procession toward the oven they have built themselves. Robert Findlay describes the finale:

> The procession evokes the image of ecstatic, self-abusing medieval flagel-lants. Continuing to sing fanatically, the group circles the black box several times. Finally the small cover of the box is removed and bright light shines up from the open pit. Each of the singing prisoners following Molik and the headless dummy leaps in frenzied fashion into this pit. Mirecka is the last,

Figure 3.5 Rena Mirecka, Ryszard Cieślak, Zygmunt Molik, Gaston Kulig, Andrzej Bielski, Mieczysław Janowski, Antoni Jahołkowski in *Akropolis* (1964). Photographer unknown, courtesy of the Archive of the Grotowski Centre, Wroclaw

and she pulls the cover closed. There is sudden silence, and a voice from the box says simply the words from Wyspiański's prologue: "They're gone and the smoke lingers on." The performance is over. The audience typically does not applaud; it simply leaves the theatre.

(Findlay 1984: 16)

Grotowski's vision was total. *Akropolis* functions on so many different levels that it is almost impossible to comprehend fully the piece in one viewing. The layers of meaning, metaphor, powerful images, and technical virtuosity of the ensemble might be perceived as too challenging for today's spoon-fed audience. However, after seeing the performance in New York in 1969, American writer J. Schevill wrote: "I know now why there is a strange joy as well as terror in crematories, and I will never escape this revelation" (cited in Kumiega 1985: 65). This kind of deep response remains the promise of the theatre—and it is Grotowski's

Theatre of Production models that continue to point the way toward a theatre that is creative, challenging, masterful, and ultimately rich in its own poverty.

PARATHEATRE EVENTS

Grotowski only spent the first 12 years or so of his professional career directing theatre productions. Throughout the 1970s, 1980s, and 1990s, he conducted other research. It would be a gross error to omit a description of some of these paratheatre activities in this discussion of Grotowski's significance as a director. Although this later work cannot be regarded as theatre production per se and it was often placed under the supervision of younger members of Grotowski's research team, his guidance is apparent and it continues to influence theatre training and thought throughout the world.

BEEHIVES

During the University of Research in 1975, one of the paratheatre activities open to all participants was called *Beehives*. *Beehives* were usually conducted in the main room of the Laboratory Theatre in Wroclaw, the same room where *Apocalypsis cum figuris* was still being performed. Seventy-five to two hundred people participated in each *Beehive*, packed into the relatively small (25 feet by 40 feet) theatre space. Several personal accounts exist about *Beehives*—especially detailed is André Gregory's account in Louis Malle's film, *My Dinner with André* (1981).

The *Beehive* was usually led by a member of the Laboratory Theatre working with a small team who guided the participants through a prearranged sequence of events. Sometimes the structure was very obvious—the participants knew exactly what to do and when to do it. Grotowski always made it clear that in any participatory event the public must first be put at ease. They should never feel coerced or confused. They must know that someone is in charge and that they will be taken care of. The so-called rules of the game must be evident to all so that the event can unfold on a fair playing field. Grotowski always looked suspiciously on attempts to fool the public into participating or on any kind of abuse of the public. For him, the more clear things were, the better the quality of participation. Again one is reminded of the *conjunctio-oppositorum*: spontaneity cannot exist without structure and to look for spontaneity without structure results in chaos and banality.

Of course, even with structure, the *Beehives* and other paratheatre activities often resulted in artificial excesses and banal behaviors. If songs were shared, participants would immediately resort to handclapping and finger snapping. They would begin to hum or sing loudly, without even hearing the song, without truly being present and receiving it. The participants often looked for a sentimental connection with the others, a group experience. All of this was too easy. The real work, in a paratheatre encounter, only began after the participants vomited these easy reactions. When people start to look for something else, a real disarmament can occur—and after that—a meeting.

Grotowski and his collaborators were aware of these problems. Applying the principle of *via negativa*, they slowly stripped away the excesses, just like they had in their theatre work. Props were eliminated. Fire, water, and other elements that were often part of the early paratheatre activities and led the participants toward clichéd behavior, were put aside. Grotowski began to envision a different kind of meeting, a meeting where nothing false gets in the way.

> When we reach the point where, in a certain space someone is drinking water, because he is thirsty, a second is singing, because he really wants to sing, a third sleeps because he really wants to sleep, a fourth is running, because something drives him to, and a fifth is fooling about, because of an interest in the others—then we are dealing with the phenomenon of the present. There is no being ahead of oneself, or behind oneself. One is where one is. This is only a first step, but it is a first step towards being what one really is... In a theatrical language we may describe this by saying that action is literal—and not symbolic, there is no division between actor and spectator, space is literal—and not symbolic.
>
> (Grotowski 1979: 227)

It was in his work with Jacek Zmysłowski, who directed *The Mountain Project* and *Vigil*, that Grotowski arrived closer and closer to his notion of literal action where the contradiction between presence and representation, action and repetition, is abolished.

THE MOUNTAIN PROJECT

The Mountain Project consisted of three parts: *Night Vigil*, *The Way*, and *The Mountain of Flame*. The first *Night Vigil* took place in September 1976 in the Laboratory Theatre's performance space. This segment functioned as a practical method to determine the participant's readiness to undertake the next phases of the project. Kumiega says, "If the *Night Vigil* can be seen as an awakening, the awakened are recognized, and the sleepers, untouched, sleep on" (Kumiega 1978: 242). The next two phases of *The Mountain Project* unfolded through the end of July 1977. Upon the completion of *The Mountain Project*, Zmysłowski selected an international team to continue working on a variation of *Night Vigil*, simply called *Vigil* (*Czuwania*). Jairo Cuesta was a member of this group and presents his recollection of the project here.

CZUWANIA (VIGIL): A RECOLLECTION

The path of the project of *Czuwania* was simple. First, we needed to confront silence, let movement arise from this silence, and only then, through this movement, meet the others. It seems simple, but on the path we had to overcome many obstacles. Silence was not just to avoid talking. It became a way to communicate with the others, to communicate the sense of the experience of the here and now. Perhaps we can talk about it more like a sense of complicity. For example, when you are on an expedition in the forest or high in the mountains, you don't need to be called. You are there when the others need you.

During the preparations for *Czuwania*, Jacek [Zmysłowski] was able to create a space of silence, where each team member found the freedom to connect with the core of silence in him or her self. Once that was accomplished, a kind of simplicity and heightened state of attention arose in each of us. I still remember the taste of the Polish bread, the sound of a guitar, the smiles of my companions in repose, and someone uttering the name of an old friend who appeared at the door.

Only when this level of silence and attention was attained did we descend to the room below—the old, empty room of the theatre. And there, patiently, we let the movement arise from our own silence.

Each of us had his or her own way. We were all so different from each other—Japanese, American, French, Colombian, German—even the six Polish members of the team were different from each other. Perhaps we can say it was like a fire built of different pieces of dried wood found in an old forest: some will burst into flames, others will fight the humidity before beginning to burn, and others will emanate some scent before any combustion is observed. In the same way, to begin the *Vigil*, some of us would just breathe or walk; others stay lying on the floor or start a series of very delicate rolls. Some of us would find a continuous flow in their movements or change from sitting to other positions of the body, testing each one as if experiencing it for the first time. Sometimes we were predictable in our reactions and other times the surprise of seeing someone go through a very strange flow of movements made us react with an even more surprising experience of our own movements. When this chain of surprising flow of movement appeared in the room, we knew we were ready for the next stage of the action: to meet the others.

Outside participants joined us in the already found space of silence. Each group of new participants had its own nature and the path toward movement was always different. Jacek [Zmysłowski] was aware of that and he was able to lead the team through different strategies of working in the space that would allow for the participants to join organically the road to movement. This process could take a lot of time—sometimes several hours—because the participants were often surprised or even scared of this non-habitual space of silence. They needed first to trust the group and then to trust themselves. When this happened they could do extraordinary things, knowing that the group was always there to support them. And when all the conditions were in place, the meeting could occur.

Grotowski found Zmysłowski's work on *Czuwania* to be a fundamental part of the paratheatre experiment:

> Jacek always insisted on the fact that what counts in the work are the extremely simple things: the movement and the space—the body and the space—the body and the movement. Nothing more, really nothing more, no miracle, no mystery, no metaphysics, no spirits, only the most simple things. In his explanations to his collaborators he always underlined the fact that it is necessary to accept certain limits and especially physical limits; for example we know that we cannot fly, so we don't speak about how to fly.
>
> (Grotowski cited in Kahn 1997: 230)

Grotowski drew much from the *Czuwania* experiment. It became an essential part of his work during Objective Drama and influenced the development of the exercise *Watching* (see Chapter 4). *Vigil* also served to verify many of Grotowski's ideas about disarmament, flow, meeting, and untaming. It remains one of the best examples from the paratheatre research of an activity that functioned on the level of **action is literal**.

ACTION: THE FINAL OPUS

It is impossible to write about Grotowski as director without some mention of the opus *Action*. This work was developed inside the project Ritual Arts or Art as Vehicle, the final phase of Grotowski's research. In the beginning of his career as a stage director, Grotowski was very upfront about his desire to create new rituals in the theatre. However, he soon abandoned that notion and decided that it was impossible to create a ritual that literally involved the spectators. He rejected theatre production and began to test his ideas in a broader arena. But even in his paratheatre experiments he discovered how difficult it is to avoid the clichés of spontaneity when working with uninitiated participants. The endpoint of the arc of his research was a structure created solely for those doing it—a structure that functioned as a vehicle for work on oneself. Lisa Wolford points out that:

> Art as vehicle is not a mimetic enactment of ritual performance; *it is ritual*...For the performer, the inner process (if, by an act of grace, it should appear) is actual. It is a manifestation of Grace.
>
> (Schechner and Wolford 2001: 15–16)

Just as his theatre production of *Akropolis* actualized the essence of the concentration camp in the here and now, it can be argued that in *Action* Grotowski's main collaborator, Thomas Richards, actualizes ritual.

Action is a ritual for those doing it: a structure in which—through a cycle of ancient songs—the doer enters into a process to transform his vital, coarse, daily-life energy to a finer, more subtle energy. It is a journey in verticality, moving upward and then back down. Because, once the energy has been transformed, the doer attempts to bring this subtle energy back into the reality of the "density" of his body and physical surroundings. It becomes, as Grotowski describes it, "All like a vertical line, and this verticality should be held taut between organicity and the awareness. Awareness means the consciousness which is not linked to language (the machine for thinking), but to Presence"

(Grotowski 1993: 125). Thomas Richards later refers to this process as the "inner action" (Richards 1997: 39).

But the question for those of us working in theatre might be "So what?" Why do this ritual, why go through this process? How is it going to help me be a better actor, play Hamlet or sing an aria? For the doer, *Action* functions as a way of working on oneself—in the true Stanislavsky meaning of the term. But for those of us in the theatre, just to witness this work can also be meaningful. It can serve as a demonstration of what is possible. Grotowski, working much like the monks in the Middle Ages copying ancient texts, has kept a flame of knowledge alive. In witnessing this work, either in person or in a filmed version, we are reminded of the craft tradition, the importance of precision, the difference between artificiality and organicity, the actualization of Presence. Here James Slowiak recalls his own confrontation with *Action*:

On a trip back to Pontedera several years after I had begun my own work, two things confronted me: Truth and Deepness. There is no masking in Grotowski's work. One faces reality, the hard, practical questions. You can't hide behind beauty, aesthetics, symbolism, or philosophy. In the Workcenter's opus, *Action*, there is no spectacle. It is pure work—work with the essentials, distilling, and deepening, a demonstration of the human spirit in action. Yes, it's not just about the body. There is that other element. But how do we approach it? How do we unblock it? How do we let it flow? That is our work, that is our craft. And first, yes, it must be approached through the body, through technique and precision—through clean action— and then perhaps it can arrive. But after this precision is achieved, something else takes over—one could call it no-precision and this is the Act. Call it Theatre of Sources, Objective Drama, Ritual Arts, Art as Vehicle, call it what you will, but the fact is that Grotowski, with the collaboration of Thomas Richards, accomplished it. It is not something that all of us need to run out and do. Grotowski never preached that his way was the only way to approach theatre. But the fact that he accomplished his goals will reverberate throughout our profession for years to come.

(Slowiak 2000b: 40)

In a text written during the last year of his life, Grotowski emphasizes Thomas Richards' exclusive authorship of *Action* (Grotowski 1999: 12). He concludes that the collaboration between them can only be understood in the sense of **transmission**—"to transmit to him [Richards] that to which I have arrived in my life: the *inner* aspect of the work" (Grotowski 1999: 12). Grotowski identifies himself as the heir of a tradition and feels a duty to transmit his knowledge to a new generation. His final questions are: "What part has research in a tradition? To what extent should a tradition of a work on oneself or, to speak by analogy, of a yoga or an inner life be at the same time an investigation, a research that takes with each new generation a step ahead?" (Grotowski 1999: 12). He considers Thomas Richards' work in the domain of art as vehicle (*Action*) to have surpassed already his own. In this final text, we are confronted once more with many of the topics that absorbed Grotowski throughout his career—from his early fascination with *yurodiviy* (holy fools) to his thorough inquiry into the nature of acting; from his wanderings through traditions and cultures to his monastic seclusion in Italy; from his radical explorations inside his laboratory to his far-reaching search beyond the borders of theatre—Grotowski never stopped asking "who-am-I?"

4

PRACTICAL EXERCISES

Grotowski was always, in all matters, a practical being. At public meetings, he often admonished young actors for their confusion or inaction with one of his favorite aphorisms: when you don't know what to do, just do. It is only in the doing that understanding can occur. The path of craft is built on attempts and failures. The first step is to enter the space and discover your capabilities.

In our work with New World Performance Laboratory, we have devised workshops based on Grotowski's principles. Some of the exercises described here come directly from our years of work with Grotowski, while other exercises grew out of our own experience working with actors around the world. All of the exercises serve one purpose: to create conditions where actors can attempt to eliminate any disturbing elements that prevent them from accomplishing four essential actions: to see, to listen, to reveal, and to meet.

PREPARATIONS

THE SPACE

Before work can start, an appropriate space must be found. Grotowski taught that difficulty in finding a workspace should never be used as a justification to delay the beginning of the work. Any space can give the possibility to work on one's craft and on oneself. However, once a workspace is selected a series of ethical questions must be answered in order to transform the chosen space into something special, a so-called sacred space.

First, the space must be clean, devoid of any distracting elements. When Grotowski conducted a workshop at Peter Brook's invitation for the Royal Shakespeare Company in the mid-1960s, the shocked British actors spent a good part of the first day cleaning the stage. The usual clutter of stages, studios, and acting classrooms made Grotowski shudder. How to create in an atmosphere of junk and leftovers? How to confront oneself in a space full of places to hide? Throughout our years of work with Grotowski, cleaning became a daily chore. No work could begin until the space sparkled. In our company, New World Performance Laboratory, we try to leave any workspace in better condition than we found it. Our actors often mop floors, wash windows, lug platforms and flats, and sweep and dust. The care of the workspace is an important element in the creation of quality.

THE SILENCE

Other principles we emphasize at the start of a workshop involve the participants' behavior. We usually ask them to put aside social habits and mannerisms:

> An act of creation has nothing to do with either external comfort or conventional human civility; that is to say, working conditions in which everybody is happy. It demands a maximum of silence and a minimum of words.
>
> (Grotowski 2002: 258)

Grotowski often lamented the modern student's need to be entertained. The aim of a workshop should not be to have fun. Everyone must be prepared to work. Leave all giggling, jokes, social chatter, and intellectualizing outside the workspace. There is a time and place for comments, questions, and analysis, and it usually is *not* during a work session. Put all attention to the task at hand, to the exercises or creative propositions. If something is not clear, continue to do, until either the instructor makes it clear or you discover for yourself the solution, the way to proceed. Never stop an exercise or interrupt a process to ask a question, comment, or reflect on what is happening. Keep doing.

Adhering to these principles creates a quality of silence that is rare in modern society and the acceptance of this silence can be a major catalyst toward transformation. Just as the exterior space must be free of clutter, so, too, the actor's interior space must empty itself of trivialities. This can be accomplished in very simple ways: forbid any social chatter in the workspace; maintain silence even during breaks or pauses; curtail any discussion among observers. In fact, don't even allow observers! Silence is a principle that appears throughout all the different phases of Grotowski's research. He often measured the quality of work by the quality of silence attained.

During his Collège de France lectures in 1997, Grotowski projected the film of Ryszard Cieślak teaching some of the Laboratory Theatre's physical exercises. Grotowski comments on Cieślak's use of silence as an instructor. Grotowski states that a bad instructor talks a lot and tries to describe the results of the exercises, what should happen. Cieślak, on the other hand, speaks rarely to the students and approaches them with silence and fluidity. He demonstrates the exercises silently, using touch and careful observation to make corrections or guide them in making discoveries. The work is a process, not a result-driven class in skills.

Sometimes Grotowski's demand for silence has been mistaken as reluctance on his part to engage in discourse about his work. This is not true. Grotowski was very open to discussion about his research and to analysis of the work being done. Such non-silent activities needed to occur, however, at the appropriate time and place and could never be automatic or mixed up with the practical work itself.

THE ACTOR'S BODY

In *Towards a Poor Theatre*, Grotowski states very clearly: "Something stimulates you and you react: that is the whole secret" (Grotowski 2002: 185). Can it get simpler? Grotowski's version of the acting process might be broken down into something like this:

Stimulation–Impulse–Action–Contact

The problem, however, is that actors' bodies seldom are receptive to stimulations; or if they happen to receive the stimulus, something blocks the flow of impulses; and if the impulses do occur, often the actor does not know how to channel these impulses into precise actions or forms in order to make contact with a partner.

Therefore, after the space has been prepared and the rules of behavior have been clarified, the workshop participant needs to "grasp the fact that nobody here wants *to give* him anything; instead they plan *to take* a lot from him . . . " (Grotowski 2002: 262). It is this "taking away" that leads toward an inductive technique, a technique of elimination, the *via negativa*.

> The education of an actor in our theatre is not a matter of teaching him something; we attempt to eliminate his organism's resistance to this psychic process. The result is freedom from the time-lapse between inner impulse and outer reaction in such a way that the impulse is already an outer reaction. Impulse and action are concurrent; the body vanishes, burns, and the spectator sees only a series of visible impulses.
>
> (Grotowski 2002: 16)

Throughout the various periods of his research, Grotowski applied the principle of *via negativa*. Whether striving toward a poor theatre, to be in the beginning (Theatre of Sources), or the unrepresentable origin (Art as Vehicle), the main principle that guided his work was the process of stripping away the non-essential to reach pure presence. But how is this done?

One must first determine how the actor relates to his/her own body. In order to eliminate the body's resistances, "The actor should be able to decipher all the problems of his body which are accessible to him" (Grotowski 2002: 35). The exercises of the Polish Laboratory Theatre described in *Towards a Poor Theatre* were developed more than 30 years ago, by a specific group of actors, from a specific culture, and in a specific time and place. Today's actors have different needs. Perception and knowledge of the human body has changed in the last 30 or 40 years. In-depth research has been conducted in movement theory, voice work, and body–mind relationship (much of it stimulated by Grotowski's investigations). A lot more information is available now than was available to Grotowski and his colleagues during the period of their initial forays into physical and vocal exercises for the actor. Grotowski even admitted in the late 1990s that it was impossible to use the same exercises with the young actors at his Workcenter in Italy that he used with his actors in Poland. To overcome the resistances, the so-called psychophysical blocks, present in our bodies today requires a different strategy. The individual's relationship with the body has changed; the predominance of machines, computers, and an image-saturated media in twenty-first-century lives creates its own plethora of psychophysical blocks. Therefore, in our workshops we begin "to get to know the body" and awake an active attention with exercises in Body Mapping and yoga stretches.

A note on garments: For most of the following exercises, participants are asked to work barefoot. Each participant should have separate garments for physical exercises (preferably a swimsuit), voice work, and creative work. Don't mix training clothes with creative work clothes. Don't sing in the same clothes you exercise in. Each type of exercise requires a specific kind of garment.

Exercise 4.1: Body Mapping

Very often the imagination we have of our bodies has little to do with the reality of our anatomy. These misconceptions can create physical habits that prevent us from maintaining "a state of idle readiness, a passive availability, which makes possible an active acting score" (Grotowski 2002: 37). Begin by asking participants some basic questions about their bodies. Where is the middle of your body? If all your flesh were stripped away and all that remained was the skeleton and we folded the skeleton in half, where would the bend occur? The answer is at the hip joint, but many people think the halfway point is the waist or navel area, or the sternum, or the pelvic bones. A wrong answer clearly indicates how separated the person is from the reality of her body. It can also demonstrate the seat of excess tensions in the body or other chronic physiological problems. Further questions can be developed to continue the mapping session:

Where is the top of your spine? Where is the bottom of your spine? Where is the hip joint, the knee joint, the ankle joint? Not in general, but precisely where does the articulation occur? If the fingers are one end of the arm structure, where is the other end? (Hint: the answer here is not the shoulder.) Where are the lungs located? How high up or how low do they go? How much does your head weigh?

Grotowski understood that actors have many blocks, not only physical blocks, but also in terms of their attitude toward their own bodies. Being ashamed of your body or narcissistic toward it both indicate a lack of acceptance of your body. You divide yourself into "me" and "my body" and this attitude creates a feeling of insecurity, a lack of trust in the body, and, therefore, a lack of trust in oneself. By spending time mapping the body and awaking an active attention, the actor begins to know her body and accept herself. "Not trusting your body means not having confidence in yourself: to be divided. *Not to be divided*: is not just the actor's seed of creativity, but is also the seed of life, of the possible whole" (Grotowski 1971a: 9).

THE SPINE

The actor who applies Grotowski's principles to training and performance must be aware that "All true reaction begins inside the body" (Grotowski 1971a: 7). Grotowski identified the source of this reaction as "la croix" (the cross); that part of the body comprising the lower part of the spinal column (the coccyx) as well as the whole base of the trunk up to and including the abdomen. In later years, Grotowski would refer to this area as "the sacrum–pelvis complex" (Grotowski 1989: 297). Engagement and unblocking of this area is essential for a body to live and react truthfully. However, Grotowski warned that this discovery must never be applied like a recipe:

> That's where the impulses begin [la croix]. You can be relatively conscious of this fact in order to unblock it, but it is not an absolute truth and must not be manipulated during exercises and never during performance. Our entire body is one big memory and in our body-memory originate various points of departure. But because this organic base of body reaction is, in a certain sense, objective, if it is blocked during exercises, it will be blocked during performance, and it will also block all of the body-memory's other departure points.
>
> (Grotowski 1971a: 7)

Throughout Grotowski's research, exercises were developed to work on engagement of the sacrum–pelvis complex and flexibility of the spinal column. Two of the most important exercises need to be mentioned here: The Cat and The Motions.

Exercise 4.2: The Cat (based on the description in *Towards a Poor Theatre*)

This exercise is based on the observation of a cat as it awakes and stretches itself. The subject lies stretched out face downwards, completely relaxed. The legs are apart and the arms at right angles to the body, palms toward the floor. The "cat" wakes up and draws the hands in toward the chest, keeping the elbows upwards, so that the palms of the hands form a basis for support. Slowly reach up with the head, wiggling the spine from side to side. When you've stretched to your limit, raise the hips up stretching the spine with support of arms and legs. Describe big circles with the pelvis. Stop the circling. Keep your right hip near the floor, placing the weight in your arms and right leg and extend the left leg out sideways away from you. Change sides and repeat the sideways stretching with your right leg. Come back to the spine stretch with the support of legs and arms. Then allow an active reaching through the top of the head to initiate a new movement, pulling the head and spine in a long curve forward along the floor. The chest, abdomen, and thighs will at first be drawn close to the floor, but as the head reaches up and forward the whole spine will be pulled into extension and onto the support of the hands. The initiation of the movement by the eyes and the follow-through are important here. On the return, initiate the movement with the tailbone as the thighs, then the abdomen, and then the chest moves close to floor. Finish the exercise by turning over and falling onto the back, relaxing.

THE MOTIONS

The Motions is a very demanding exercise developed during the period of Theatre of Sources and further refined during Objective Drama and Art as Vehicle. The exercise consists of the "primal position" and a series of stretches. The primal position is "a position of the body in which the spine is slightly inclined, the knees slightly bent, a position held at the base of the body by the sacrum–pelvis complex..." (Grotowski 1989: 297). Thomas Richards describes the structure of the exercise thus:

The stretches are simple (one can see some similarities to hatha yoga, but it is different). There are three cycles of stretches/positions. Each cycle is one specific stretch/position executed four times, once toward each of the cardinal directions; turning from one direction to the next is done standing on the same spot. Separating each cycle is a stretch called nadir/zenith, a quick stretch down followed by a quick one up.

(Richards 1995: 54)

Even though The Motions is an exercise that can be learned superficially in a few sessions, its many challenges require systematic work over a long period of time, under the tutelage of someone who has mastered the exercise, in order to execute it with consciousness of all its levels. Primarily, it is an exercise in synchronization of details within a group and in "circulation of attention," in seeing. "You must see what is before you and hear what is around you in each moment of the exercise. And in the same time be present to your own body: 'see that you are seeing, hear that you are hearing'" (Richards 1995: 55).

One can say that all exercises based on Grotowski's principles are intended to create this particular acceptance of the present, this process of "not to be divided." While The Motions must be learned from someone who has mastered the exercise, one can approach "presence" in simpler ways as well. Just begin by being in the space. Don't imagine the space as someplace else. If it's a room, you are in the room. And what is happening is happening. This can be the departure point for any number of exercises.

THE ACTOR'S PRESENCE: TO SEE

Exercise 4.3: attention to space

Begin by walking around the room. At first, be aware of the decisions needed to change directions. Keep going. This will awaken the organism's urge to make itself known. Movement is assertion. Be aware of how you are placing your feet on the ground. There should be no noise of footsteps. Grotowski would often say the easiest way to tell a professional from an amateur is by how much noise they make when walking. No noise. By trying not to make noise, the actor is already in a higher state of attention. Remember that walking is an exercise in shifting balance from one leg to the other. Don't repeat the same step mechanically. Observe how each step is different depending on the stimulation from the space and the others in the space. Don't repeat the same pattern in the space over and over. See your partners.

Don't fix your look on the floor. Don't make 'faces' at your partners: social smiles, flirtations, eye rollings, or other social masks. At every moment you should know where your partners are in the room. You should navigate between them as a captain guides his boat on the tranquility of the ocean surface avoiding all the dangerous places he knows are under the surface. Just try to find an easy, light, and free walk around the room. The golden rule is always to go toward the empty space. Serve your partners. Give them the space they need to work. When the space is "controlled," you and your partners will have the clear sensation of being like swallows flying in groups of hundreds in the sky, never colliding.

THE ACTOR AS HUNTER

When control of the space arrives to this certain quality (there are no collisions and the group is moving as one organism), continue to work on raising the group's level of attention, their state of presence, as a whole, and as individuals. Here we often introduce exercises for a kind of attention that we call "horizontal" attention. Horizontal attention involves a merging of action and awareness, a basic element of the experience of space.

Very often you hear directors or teachers crying out, "Use the space." Befuddled actors look at each other wondering, "What does she want me to do?" Before actors can use the space, they must know how to experience the space. But how do actors learn to experience the space? They must be stimulated to activate a diffuse or peripheral awareness, which can be characterized as being horizontal in nature and requires a very high level of trust. It is a kind of awareness similar to the attention of the hunter:

The hunter does not believe that he knows where the critical moment is going to occur. He does not look tranquilly in one determined direction, sure beforehand that the game will pass in front of him. The hunter knows that he does not know what is going to happen, and this is one of the greatest attractions of his occupation. Thus he needs to prepare an attention of a different and superior style—an attention which does not consist in riveting itself on the presumed but consists precisely in not presuming anything and in avoiding inattentiveness. It is a "universal" attention, which does not inscribe itself on any point and tries to be on all points. There is a magnificent term for this, one that still conserves all its zest of vivacity and imminence: alertness. The hunter is the alert man.

(Ortega y Gasset 1972: 150)

The actor in Grotowski's theatre is the "alert man."

Exercise 4.4: the sticks

Introduce a stick (the size of broom handle or smaller) into the previous exercise of Control of the Space. Without losing the quality of attention previously attained, begin to give and to receive the stick from one actor to another. Hunt for the right moment to give and be ready to receive. Don't attach to the stick. Pass it as quickly as you can. The stick burns. It is a hot potato. Be aware of the weight of the stick. Hold it always in its center and keep it vertical. Otherwise, it may be dangerous for the others. The stick should never fall to the floor. It must always be given and received. The walking accelerates into running and the passing becomes an easy throwing. When the stick is moving rapidly from hand to hand, you can introduce others until the number of sticks equals the number of actors in the space.

When all is working well, introduce the voice. Begin a counting game. The group must count from 1 to 20. Only one voice for each number. If two actors call out the same number at the same time, the group needs to come back to the beginning. (e.g. 1; 2; 3; 4, 4, back to 1). If a stick is dropped in the middle of counting, the group must also begin the count again. When the group arrives to 20, one stick can be taken out and the game continues. The running doesn't stop until all the sticks have been taken out. This exercise can undergo many variations as the group becomes more proficient and adapts to working together. The exercise presents a challenge on many levels, not only for attention, but also for stamina, contact, rhythm, and trust. It is a simple and immediate way to activate horizontal attention and an experience of space.

UNTAMING

At this point the actor's body should be more open to stimulations, both from the outside and from within the sphere of their own being, the so-called **inner world**. What is the next step? In many training programs, the actors would now begin to learn some kind of technique. Perhaps acrobatics or calisthenics or some mime or dance steps would be introduced. Grotowski opposed this kind of actor training. He felt such training does not liberate the body, but rather imprisons it within a fixed number of movements and reactions. "If only some movements are perfected, then all the others remain underdeveloped. The body is not freed. The body is tamed . . . What must be done is to free the body, not just train certain areas. But to give the body a chance. To give it the possibility to live and to be radiant, to be personal" (Grotowski 1971a: 5–6). We now encounter the principle that Grotowski has referred to as **untaming**.

> In seeking an original state we have two possibilities. The first possibility is by means of a training which will be later abolished. As in the art of the Samurai: there must first take place a conscious mastery, then practically on the principle of a conditioned reflex, and finally a mastery of the warrior's skills. But at the point that he becomes a real warrior, he must forget everything. The second possibility is through untaming. From the moment we are born we are tamed in everything: how to see, how to hear, what is what, how to be, how to eat, how to drink water, what is possible and what is impossible . . . And so the second possibility is to untame the tamed. This is very difficult work. Untaming demands greater effort and self-discipline than training.
>
> (Grotowski cited in Kumiega 1985: 228–9)

For Grotowski, the first technique was both understandable and respectable. However, he believed that in a technological society investigation of the second technique, untaming, creates more equilibrium. Therefore, all the exercises he proposed, even the most structured, have as their purpose to untame the actor's body.

Jacek Zmysłowski led an international group of young people during a special project in Wroclaw beginning in 1977. This project came to be called *Czuwania (The Vigil)*. *Czuwania* was enacted over a period of several years in various locations with the leading team and participants. Zmysłowski was interested in the relation between space, movement, and body. "In this action there is only empty space, the people who arrive, and nothing else. Very simple things happen in this time, but simple in the sense that everyone has the capacity to do something in the space, in this room" (Zmysłowski cited in Kahn 1997: 227). Silence was another element that complemented the experience. No voice, no verbal communication was needed to allow for the possibility to create different relations with people both known and unknown. "But because it is so simple, sometimes it is very difficult to take the first step" (Zmysłowski cited in Kahn 1997: 227).

How to take the first step? This was the question that Grotowski tried to answer with Jairo Cuesta many years later in California during Objective Drama in 1985. Here the work began by first recalling the different strategies the *Czuwania* group used with participants. Cuesta led the Irvine group through many long hours of work and eventually a structure emerged which was named Watching.

Exercise 4.5: Watching

At first glance, Watching looks like a game of follow the leader. In reality, however, the structure functions to give participants the freedom to follow their own stream or flow while executing the technical aspects with precision. Watching works as an exercise based on *conjunctio-oppositorum* (the conjunction of opposites). In this case, the opposites are structure and spontaneity. But Watching also tests the participant's quality of attention. The primary objective is to watch, as the name suggests. You can't go to sleep. Wake up and watch. But watch actively, through movement.

The ideal place to do Watching is an open space outdoors or an empty room where there is enough space to accomplish each of the tasks required. The group can range from three to more than twenty, depending on the size of the space. In the early days, the exercise often lasted for three hours or more. Presently, Watching takes about 25 minutes.

Watching consists of ten different sections. Each section has its own dynamic and duration. Only when the leader acknowledges that the group has accomplished the task for each section can they pass to the next one. Watching is a silent activity. No cries, moans, or verbalizations. No stomping, pounding, or drumming. No flailing arms, pseudo-fits, acrobatics, or choreography. Don't do what you know how to do. Look for what you don't know how to do.

To begin, the participants place themselves in front of the space in a line. Already this position is part of the work. Each person embodies a state of readiness.

Section # 1: Control of the Space

When the leader enters the space, all the participants follow. The group functions as one. The task is to place yourself in the space and in relation to the other participants in such a way that the entire room is balanced: no big empty spaces; not everyone in the center or on the periphery; not forming a big circle. Each participant, with their own dynamics, must work in coordination with the entire group to find their place simultaneously. The next step is to crouch in an active position. This position is a kind of squat with the weight more on one foot so the other foot can serve as a pivot for an eventual displacement. The hands and knees should not be in contact with the floor.

Control of the Space is composed of three moments:

A   Immobility. To see. To listen. To be ready. Sense the flow of movement inside you and let it slowly appear. Control the space with only your eyes.

B   Movement without displacement. You see; you listen. You open your attention to the environment, to the others. Do you really know this place? Do you really see your partners? Small movements begin. You look in different directions. You see everything you can see without changing location or standing. Notice how your weight shifts.

C   Displacement in the space. Keeping the active squat position you begin to explore the space around you. You change location and react to the displacement of the others. Remember to control the space. Always serve the space. Always serve your partners. Eventually the group finds the right moment to stand up.

Section # 2: The Web

The group begins to pattern a web in the space. The Web also consists of three moments. However, they are much longer in duration:

A   Pulsation. Once standing, each participant goes directly to the periphery in order to form a well-balanced circle with the whole group. The group begins moving together, each individual taking a straight path toward the center where they meet at the same time. After the meeting, each person chooses a new direction to go, taking them to a new location on the periphery. This movement evolves into a group pulsation between the periphery and the center. The challenge in this section is always to form a balanced circle on the periphery and always to meet together in the center. A straight path must be used from the center to the periphery and vice versa. Never allow yourself to doubt or change your mind when you go to the periphery. If the space is not balanced on the first few attempts, stick to the rules. Eventually, the group will discover the necessary degree of coordination and attention so that the circle on the periphery is always well balanced. Avoid any collisions. Don't be late. Work as a group and watch the leader. Don't give in to fatigue this early in the exercise. A high level of complicity within the group will make the coordination work. When the pulsation is beating at a constant rhythm (almost by itself), the leader signals the shift to the second moment of The Web.

B   Crescent-moons. This movement begins from the periphery. Without changing the dynamic attained in pulsations, the leader initiates a new path in the space instead of going toward the center. The leader moves in a semicircle toward the right or the left of her last position on the periphery. The group follows, without stopping or cutting their flow in any way, and begins to play with the space by forming a series of different crescent-moon orbits around a unique center. Note: it is not a whole circle orbit, but a half-circle orbit, at different distances from the center. The individual traces a half-circle in the space, returning via the same path to the starting point or beginning a new orbit, smaller or bigger than the preceding one. This continuous change of orbits and directions, using only half-circle orbits, creates the horizontal lines of a web, connecting the vertical lines previously formed by the pulsations. It also establishes a kind of planetary movement around the center in which we can imagine each participant as a different planet with its own orbit around the sun. What are the challenges? No crashes. No straight lines. Balance the space: the crescent-moon orbits should not all be near the center or all on the periphery. Play the game: remember you are serving the space; remember you are watching. When should you move to another orbit? In reaction to whom? How can the group work together to create the dynamic of this section? After these basic questions are answered you can begin to look for more individual ways of moving within the crescent-moon structure. This shift to Individual Crescent-Moons serves as the catalyst into the next section. When the group has attained a high level of complicity and coordination, the leader signals the change into the third moment of The Web.

C   Silent Dance. The leader must be very attentive to choose when to propose the beginning of Silent Dance. The space needs to be well balanced at the climax of Crescent-moons so that, at the moment of passage from one section to the next, each participant finds him/herself in a different location in the space. Again, attention to not form a circle or have everyone in the center, etc. The Web has been constructed in order for Silent Dance to occur. Silent Dance is a simple dance in one spot. There is no change of location during Silent Dance. It is silent, but everyone is dancing to the same music: the whisper of footsteps, the sounds of respiration. Eyes are open. The search is for your own dance. Look for how you danced before you learned how to dance. Look for your child-dance, your first dance. You are alone and yet dancing with the others in the same place, to the same silent music. Don't be heavy. Don't attach to a way of dancing. Don't repeat mechanically some movement. Remember the questions are important, not the answers. The answers will come in the doing. Follow your process. Don't stop. Just go deep in your dance.

When the Silent Dance reaches its climax, the leader begins to run.

Section # 3: Running

From wherever you are in Silent Dance, the whole group simultaneously follows the leader and begins to run in a big circle around the periphery of the space. The running is counterclockwise. It is running, not jogging. The arms are not chugging—they are relaxed. The group is like a herd of wild horses running together. Look for the complicity of wild horses. No noise. No stomping. No calling. No heavy breathing. Sometimes you may be the locomotive for your partners; sometimes you may be alone and yet in coordination with the others. Let your body run. Don't make it run. Run with a purpose. Run toward something or away from something important to you. You can pass the others, but do it on the outside. Otherwise, just run.

Section # 4: Nebula

When the running reaches its peak and the group has gone on to its second or third wind, the circular path begins to move toward the center until the group is running, with the same speed and dynamic, in a very tight circle around the center. At this moment, from within the newly formed nebula, there is an explosion into **individual stars**. Individual stars means that the running circle, the tight nebula, disperses in all directions, so that each participant arrives to a different place in the space, balancing the space, once again, avoiding forming a circle. At this moment, the next section begins.

Section # 5: Silent Dance II

Silent Dance II takes place within the same parameters as the first Silent Dance. However, this time the dance is directed toward someone in the room, almost as an offering. There is no need to acknowledge to whom the dance is directed. Just offer it. Be aware not to stop the process. If the first Silent Dance was about contact with the space, Silent Dance II becomes about contact with the partner, from a distance. When the leader determines it's time, the group passes to the next section.

Section # 6: Pulsation II

Technically, Pulsation II is the same as the first Pulsation. From the various locations of Silent Dance II, the group meets in the center and then goes to the periphery. The group continues to work the skills of attention, coordination, balance of the space, complicity, silence, stamina, and being in harmony with the environment. However, here, too, the focus has now shifted somewhat from the space to the partners. More attention now is directed toward the others. The space should be taking care of itself. So this second web becomes a preparation for making contact.

Section # 7: Crescent-moons II

Again this section is enacted technically the same as the first Crescent-moons. The Pulsation II and Crescent-moons II complete the second web so the space is reorganized in order for contact to occur. During the individual crescent-moons, when a more improvised manner of making the semicircle patterns is sought, the focus is directed toward the others, hunting the possibility for a meeting. This meeting is the essence of the next section.

Section # 8: Connection–Disconnection

Connection–Disconnection is the most challenging section of Watching. Everything accomplished so far in the exercise has been leading to this moment. In this section you meet a partner; you initiate a one-on-one connection. When the leader begins to connect with someone, the group is free to abandon the crescent-moon patterns and move in relation to what is happening in the space. But how does one initiate a connection? A connection is not an imposition on someone else. Contact is established through a look or perhaps through a moment of coordinated movement or a recognized spatial relationship. It's not even that you "look for" a connection. Often they just happen. When you find yourself in connection with someone, don't begin to engage in manic movements. See each other. Approach each other. And begin to "speak" to each other through your movement. Not trivial chatter, but reveal something about yourself and try to discover something about your partner. The connection is neither a club dance nor a mirror exercise. Each of you will have your own way of moving through which you will try to contact your partner. Through your dance you will try to know who your partner is and your partner will try to discover who you are. Dance this discovery. Relish this dialogue. See something about your partner you never saw before. Tell a secret. And at the climax of the connection—you disconnect. Disconnection is the most important moment in Connection–Disconnection. Find the right moment to separate, to go away, end the meeting. Just don't do it too early, before something happens, and not too long after something happens. Don't cling to the connection. Don't attach to your partner. The élan of disconnection resembles two wild horses separating after a moment of joyful play. You return to control of the space and perhaps prepare for another Connection–Disconnection.

Some other things to remember: a connection can only occur between two persons, never three or more. There is no touching, no stopping, and no verbalization. Your connection should not disturb the connections of the others. You should not intrude on any one else's space. Even though you are in connection, you do not lose attention to the rest of the group and what is happening in the space. You must always remain vigilant. If you don't engage in a connection, focus on controlling the space.

The leader discreetly signals the passage to the next section.

Section # 9: The Spiral

At the finish of Connection–Disconnection, the group's movement dynamic evolves into a slow walk. This shift marks the beginning of The Spiral. Spiral refers to an ascending and descending dynamic. It does not describe a way of moving or a pattern in the space. At the beginning, the group moves slowly, ascending one step at a time toward a climax of speed and dynamism. Once the climax is reached, the group begins its descent, eventually finishing in a very slow movement dynamic. The challenge again lies in the control of the space (no crashes) and the coordination and complicity within the group. When the group's dynamic descends to a very slow movement, they pass to the next section.

Section # 10: Control of the Space II

The group goes down to the active, squat position that began the exercise and reverses the order of the Control of the Space section they did previously:

A   Control of the space with displacement.
B   Control of the space with movement, no displacement.
C   Immobility.

When immobility is accomplished, the group rises and leaves the space. Watching is finished.

Watching touches many principles of both group and individual work. When the exercise is repeated, an actor's movement habits and psychophysical obstacles become apparent immediately. Actors who work without consideration for the others or always try to be in the limelight are exposed. The actor's box of tricks does not work in

Watching. It is not an improvisation (in the usual meaning of that word). It is not a license for free expression or pumping emotion. It is a structure to seek truthful, organic movement and pure, honest meetings between partners. Other exercises also work toward this kind of untaming and organicity. Some of them involve more precise technical elements than Watching and must be worked over a long period of time. Among these exercises are The Plastiques and The Corporals, two distinct trainings developed during the first 10 years of Grotowski's research into the actor's craft (Figure 4.1).

PRECISION

The Plastiques and The Corporals are the exercises for which the Laboratory Theatre became famous throughout the world and are described in *Towards a Poor Theatre*. Here we will outline some of the important principles governing these now-classic exercises and demonstrate how to use these principles to build one's own physical exercise sequence or training structure.

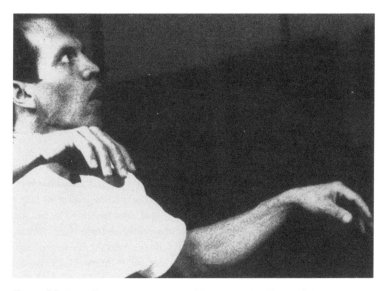

Figure 4.1 Jairo Cuesta training (2003). Photograph by Marino Colucci

In the article, "Exercises," Grotowski summarizes his conclusions on the actor's physical training:

> I believe that in all the problems of exercises the misunderstanding stems from the initial error that to develop the different parts of the body will free the actor, will liberate his expression. It's just not true. You should not "train" and, because of that, even the word "training" is not right. You should not train, not in a gymnastic way or in an acrobatic way, not with dance nor with gestures. Instead, working apart from rehearsals, you should confront the actor with the seeds of creativity.
>
> (Grotowski 1971a: 6)

The Plastiques were developed from well-known systems such as **Delsarte**, **Dalcroze**, European pantomime, and others.

Francois Delsarte (1811–71): French acting and singing teacher who emphasized a connection between physical state and mental/emotional attitude. His findings were codified into a system of gestures for use by actors and dancers.

Emile-Jacques Dalcroze (1865–1950): Swiss musician and educator who developed Eurythmics, a method that incorporates body movement in the learning of music.

Plastic exercises traditionally have worked an actor's ability to create forms. Sometimes they are referred to as "gesture" exercises. However, Grotowski and his colleagues envisioned these plastic exercises like a *conjunctio-oppositorum* between structure and spontaneity. He and his actors isolated a certain number of plastic exercises from these various systems that gave "the possibility of an organic reaction, rooted in the body, and that finds its completion in precise details" (Grotowski 1971a: 8). These details were then fixed by the actors and memorized, until they could execute them precisely, without thinking about them. The task then became to discover the personal impulses that could transform the details—transform them, but not destroy them.

> The question is this: how to begin by improvising only the order of the details, by improvising the rhythm of the fixed details, and then to change the order and the rhythm, and even the composition of the details, not in a premeditated fashion, but with the flow dictated by our own bodies?
>
> (Grotowski 1971a: 7)

The process of creating an exercise can begin with any number of fixed forms. In the Plastiques, Grotowski called these forms "details." The process can commence from other points, with a completely different set of details. No matter how one begins, it takes a long period of selection, eliminating those forms or details that are too artificial or aesthetic or block the flow of impulses and the body-life.

The Corporal exercises were developed in much the same manner, only here the departure point was several *asanas* (especially the upside-down positions) of hatha yoga. The Corporal exercises act like a kind of challenge to one's nature. They should seem almost impossible to do, yet possible. Again there was a long period of natural selection as Grotowski refined the concrete elements of the Corporal exercises. He always stressed the importance of a clear groundwork, mastering the precise forms, before beginning to vary the physical exercises.

Only after this period of embodiment can one begin to improvise and seek something else, but all the while, keeping the concrete elements: "In the corporal exercises, you must keep the concrete elements, just like you keep the precision in the plastic exercises. Without concreteness, cheating begins, rolling on the ground, chaotic movements, convulsions, and all this done with the conviction that these are exercises" (Grotowski 1971a: 10). The key in the Corporals is to "not prevent yourself" from doing the exercises. Let your nature guide you. Equilibrium becomes the symptom of a primitive trust and confidence in your own body. Again: not to be divided. You challenge yourself and you surpass yourself.

> If you do not refuse, then, in surpassing yourself, you discover a certain trust. You begin to live. Then the *body-memory* dictates the rhythm, the order of the elements, their transformation, but the elements remain concrete. They don't turn into plasma. Here it's not a matter of the exterior precision that exists in the details of the plastic exercises, but the elements

are present and we don't dictate to ourselves the natural pulsation during the evolutions. "That" dictates itself; "that" does itself. In the end, the living contents of our past (or our future?) begin to intervene. So it is difficult to say if it's a question of exercises or much more a type of improvisation; it can be our contact with the other, with the others, with our life fulfilling itself, embodying itself in the body's evolutions. If the *body-life* wishes to guide us in another direction, we can be the beings, the space, the landscape that resides inside us, the sun, the light, the absence of light, the open or closed space—without any calculation. Everything begins to be *body-life*.

(Grotowski 1971a: 11)

The actor does not ask: "How can I do this?" Instead, the actor must know what not to do, what obstructs him from accomplishing the exercise. Each exercise adapts to the individual as he seeks solutions to eliminate the various obstacles, muscular blockages, fears, or other personal impediments. By following these principles and without merely imitating the exercises of the Polish Laboratory Theatre, any group can create its own physical exercise sequence (Figure 4.2).

Figure 4.2 NWPL Training demonstration. Poland (2002). Photograph by Douglas-Scott Goheen

Exercise 4.6: the physical exercise sequence (training)

Begin by asking each participant to select six to nine exercises that challenge their various physical weaknesses or blocks. You might divide the weaknesses thusly: Flexibility, Strength, Balance, Plasticity (the ability to hold forms), and Stamina. The exercises can come from any source. Just as Grotowski worked with hatha yoga and various plastic exercise systems, we have developed training sequences based on exercises from martial arts, Tai Chi, or even from calisthenics like sit-ups and push-ups. Once each participant has selected, memorized, and refined the particular exercises, they must transform each exercise to make it personal and dynamic. This can be done by first placing the exercises in a chain and doing them in an uninterrupted flow. Make sure any repetition is done with purpose. Nothing should be mechanical. Improvise with the space and with the order of the exercises. For example, each exercise must be performed in a different place in the space. The passage from one exercise to another should be dynamic as well and create a build and flow to the whole sequence. Work with a partner. Change the rhythm or quality of each exercise in relation to the others present in the space, in relation to an invisible partner, to what you hear, to a memory, or even some fantastic image. "A good stimulus is anything that throws you into action with all yourself and a bad stimulus is that which divides you into body and mind" (Grotowski 1974: 50, author's trans.). The physical exercise sequence should function as a kind of personal Tai Chi: a precise structure that challenges the actor's nature, yet keeps them disciplined, coherent in what they are doing. Determine what not to do. Eliminate anything that gets in the way: heaviness, fatigue, choreography, cheating, senseless repetition, beautiful forms, gestures, athleticness, wandering in the space, staring, attaching to one element, doing something only halfway. But always know what you are doing, what you are working.

> Gradually, we arrive to what we call "organic acrobatics," dictated by certain regions of the body-memory, by certain intuitions of the body-life. Each one gives birth to his way and is accepted by the others in their way. Like children who look for how to be free, how to free themselves from the bounds of space and gravity. And not through calculation. But we don't pretend to be children, because we're not children. Yet it's

possible to refind analogous sources or, maybe, even the same sources, and, without turning away from the child inside us, we can look for that "organic acrobatics" (which is not acrobatics), which is individual and refers to bright and living needs; this is possible if we have not yet begun to die, little by little, by renouncing the challenge of our own nature.

(Grotowski 1971a: 11)

Grotowski was against exercises for self-improvement. He often stated that bodybuilding or exercising merely to become more beautiful or to perfect yourself was just another form of avoidance. "If we think in categories of perfection, improvement, self-development, etc., we reaffirm today's indifference. And what does that signify? The desire to avoid the Act, to escape from what should be accomplished now, today" (Grotowski 1971a: 12). In Grotowski's world, there is no place to hide. In our work with New World Performance Laboratory, we have developed several exercises in coordination and rhythm that help to reach a state where you cannot hide.

COORDINATION AND RHYTHM

In later years, Grotowski remarked that the best training for an actor might be some form of martial arts. He pointed out that in this type of combat exercise the results are always tangible. If you don't do the right move, you get kicked. The exercise called Four Corners belongs to this family of exercises where the results are clear for the participants. Four Corners engages all your senses to such a degree that you readily establish extraordinary coordination with your partners.

In 1989, as part of New World Performance Laboratory's (NWPL) Project in Performance Ecology, we found ourselves trying to continue to work on the possibilities opened by Grotowski's principle of *conjunctio-oppositorum*. We began to work around some of Delsarte's exercises in succession, opposition, and parallelism as well as on his different Laws of Movement. We also explored Dalcroze's Eurythmic exercises. Finally, we turned to Samuel Beckett's play, *Quad*, for inspiration. We found that the spatial and rhythmical structure of the piece gave us a tool to continue our own research.

Although the exercise borrows some structural elements from Beckett's play, Four Corners is in no way a production of *Quad*.

The exercise operates as a movement exercise where four participants are challenged to accomplish perfect spatial and rhythmical coordination between them, while seeking their own inner process. It is a game where the tension between challenge and skill is harmonious and continuous.

Exercise 4.7: Four Corners

The four participants form an ample square about 15 feet x 15 feet. Each corner is the home and entrance to the square of one participant. The corners are numbered: Corner number (Cn) Cn1, Cn2, Cn3, and Cn4. Corner 1 is Down Left; Corner 2 Up Left; Corner 3 Down Right; and Corner 4 Up Right. The participants take the number of their own corner: #1, #2, #3, and #4.

We begin by learning the basic pattern: a path that leads each participant along the sides and through the diagonals of the square.

The path for #1 will be from Cn1 to Cn3 then a diagonal toward Cn2 to Cn1, then a diagonal to Cn4. From there to Cn2 followed by a diagonal to Cn3. From Cn3 to Cn4 and a new diagonal leads home to Cn1.
The path for #2 will follow the same basic pattern: Cn2; Cn1; Cn4; Cn2; Cn3; Cn4; Cn1; Cn3; Cn2.
The path for #3 will be: Cn3; Cn4; Cn1; Cn3; Cn2; Cn1; Cn4; Cn2; Cn3.
The path for #4 will be: Cn4; Cn2; Cn3; Cn4; Cn1; Cn3; Cn2; Cn1; Cn4.

When the participants are familiar with their paths, they can begin to work together. The structure is formed by four cycles and each cycle is composed of six phases: Solo, Duo, Trio, Quartet, Trio, and Duo.

#1 begins doing her path alone. This is the Solo of Cycle I. When she arrives home, she continues her path but this time in a Duo with #3. Now the work in coordination begins. The two participants need to work together, keeping their individual way of walking, running, or dancing, yet arriving to the corners and to the center in synchronization, at the same time.

Special attention must be put on how to negotiate the meeting in the center. On the diagonal path, you should always keep to your right, so there is no collision with your partner. The challenge is to find the way to be in the center at the same time as your partner. Don't avoid the center, but work in coordination with your partners to experience the risky meeting in the center.

When the meeting is a perpendicular one, observe the following rule: always let the person who approaches you from the right pass before you. And when you're in a Trio or Quartet, add the following rule: always pass before the person that approaches you from the left. *But remember: everyone must pass through the center at the same time, as close as possible to each other.*

Then Cycle I continues. When #1 and #3 arrive home, #4 joins them and the Trio of Cycle I begins. When they arrive home again, #2 joins them and the Quartet of Cycle I begins. When they all arrive home again, #1 goes out and there is a Trio involving #3, #4, and #2. At home #3 goes out and #4 and #2 have a Duo. When at home again, #4 goes out, letting #2 alone to do a Solo and thus begins Cycle II.

Cycle II follows the same general structure. After the Solo of #2, #1 enters. After the Duo, #4 enters. After the Trio, #3 enters. After the Quartet, #2 goes out. After the Trio, #1 goes out. After the Duo, #4 goes out, letting #3 alone to do a Solo and thus begins Cycle III.

Cycle III. Solo of #3; enter #2 for the Duo; enter #1 for the Trio; enter #4 for the Quartet. Exit #3; exit #2; exit #1. #4 begins a Solo that begins Cycle IV.

Cycle IV. Solo of #4; enter #3 for the Duo; enter #2 for the Trio; enter #1 for the Quartet. Exit in the following order: #4, #3, #2 and leave #1 to do a Solo and finish the exercise or begin the structure again.

It is important for the team to find complicity at the beginning of the exercise. Therefore, a solo dance performed in the corner in relation with the others can create a team preparation before the exercise properly begins (Figure 4.3). This dance can drive you through the whole structure. You can return to your dance while you are waiting for your next entrance. Your dance functions as a stimulus for your partners and, at the same time, helps you to remain active and present. When the structure is accomplished, the team finds the way to arrive to an ending through the solo dance.

THE ACTOR'S VOICE: TO LISTEN

Grotowski's primary principle for voice work is: Body first and then voice. "The most elementary fault, and that in most urgent need of correction, is the overstraining of the voice because one forgets to speak with the body" (Grotowski 2002: 185). The voice is an extension of the body. It is like

Figure 4.3 Four Corners demonstration. Italy (1989). Photograph by Deanna Frosini

another appendage, not a separate organism. The voice extends toward the exterior. It is a material force (vibration) that can even touch things. The voice can caress, stab, pinch, and tickle. To work on the voice as something apart from the body leads the actor away from his/her organic state.

It is in the field of voice work that Grotowski made many of his greatest contributions to actor-training techniques. Jennifer Kumiega states that while in the field of physical exercises there is little in the way of objective results to be passed on from the work of the Laboratory Theatre, "there have been valuable objective results in the areas of breathing and vocal training" (Kumiega 1985: 112). Many of these results seem like good common sense. For example, Grotowski identified two conditions necessary for good vocal carrying power:

1. The column of air carrying the sound must escape with force and without meeting obstacles (e.g. a closed larynx or insufficient opening of the jaw).
2. The sound must be amplified by the physiological resonators.

(Grotowski 2002: 147)

In his article, "Voice," Grotowski describes some of the other objective results and the many roads he traveled toward discovering the secrets of the vocal resonators and how to work the voice in a creative and organic manner.

RESPIRATION

Grotowski and his actors recognized three kinds of respiration:

1   Upper thoracic or pectoral respiration, which is predominant among European and American women because of cultural traditions in clothing (girdles and brassieres) and socially learned behaviors;
2   Abdominal respiration, which engages the diaphragm as its chief characteristic and allows the abdomen and lower ribs to expand (this type of respiration is most often taught and practiced in theatre schools and actor-training programs); and
3   Total respiration, which begins in the abdomen and then subtly engages the chest on a second level. Grotowski remarked that this type of respiration is most often found in babies and animals and is the most healthy and functional of the three.

Despite his belief in the naturalness of total respiration, Grotowski found that no respiration technique can be generally applied. Some actors are incapable of abdominal respiration and he berated those teachers who teach a "correct" or "normal" way to breathe. Grotowski believed that there is no "right way" to breathe and that one should only intervene in respiration if there is a clear problem, because any intervention can hinder the actor's organic process. "You should observe what is happening—if the actor has no difficulty with air, if he inhales a sufficient quantity of air when he acts, you should not intervene (Grotowski 1971b: 90). He also felt that certain vocal drills and theatre school exercises did more harm than good in eliminating vocal blocks and resolving respiration problems. For example, exercises in trying to obtain long exhalations, such as speaking a long speech on one breath or counting to 100 without taking a breath, only serve to close the larynx. The actor does fine as long as it is easy and then when it becomes difficult he tries to conserve air and unconsciously closes the larynx. Therefore, he is only practicing how to close the larynx, not how to release the voice on a strong and free flow of air.

Exercises stressing the consonants also create problems. Vocal exercises should stress the vowels. Then the larynx remains open. Consonants, which must be drilled for correct articulation, should be worked by placing a vowel before and after: "ada-ada-ada" and not "d-d-d-d." Other problems that may be observed are those actors who hold their breath during physical activity or who breathe and move in the same rhythm. If these problems are observed in training, most likely they will also occur during performance. The director or instructor should then point out the problem to the actor while being attentive not to intervene by trying to coordinate the actor's movements with his breathing or applying some kind of breathing technique.

Exercise 4.8: respiration exercises

The challenge of any respiration exercise is to find and create a situation in which the actor can discover his own, unblocked respiration process. One simple exercise is to have the actor lie on the floor on his back and breathe. That's it. Observe his body and if the abdomen is not moving, the respiration is not total. Then tell him when he begins to breathe totally. Use negative phrases rather than positive ones. Say, "Now you're *not* blocking the flow," instead of "Now you're breathing correctly, before you were breathing badly." If the actor thinks there is a *correct* way to breathe, he will try to intervene consciously and block his process. So the language is important. You can also have the actor plug one nostril to inhale and plug the other one to exhale. This exercise may allow him to discover his own respiration. However, the instructor must be attentive because the actor can also simulate total or abdominal respiration by manipulating the abdominal muscles. If the actor is inhaling by engaging the diaphragm, the bottom ribs will flare out, on the sides and in the back. This movement can be verified by touch and is much more difficult to fake than the movement of the abdominal muscles. Grotowski also suggests placing the actor in positions that are physically difficult and demand his attention, standing on his head, for example. You can also tire the actor physically through exercises until he reaches a state of fatigue. In these cases, his attention is elsewhere and he no longer interferes in his organic respiratory process.

Grotowski stresses that one should not seek an ideal model of respiration, a correct way to breathe, but look for the way to open up one's natural respiration:

> I am going to repeat again that you must wait, don't intervene too fast, wait and, instead, look for how to free the organic process through action. Because in this case—almost always by itself—the respiration will free itself, too, and, in this way, the actor will not have intervened, controlled, or blocked his respiration.
>
> (Grotowski 1971b: 95)

Respiration is individual. Each actor has his or her own blocks and uninhibited, total respiration is different for each person. This difference—no matter how small—is key when it comes to naturalness.

THE RESONATORS

The greatest adventure of Grotowski's work with the voice was the discovery of the different resonators. Most voice teachers speak about only two resonators: the head (or mask) and the chest resonators. Grotowski, however, identified at least twenty-four different resonators in the body. He felt that limiting the voice to the classic resonators led to a "typical" actor voice and a hammy sound. He observed that different languages engage different resonators. The high-pitched sound in certain

Chinese dialects emanates from the occipital joint in the nape of the neck. Certain Slavic languages use the stomach as a resonator. Germans utilize the teeth. It may seem naïve, but if one directs the voice to these different points in the body, an actual vibration occurs in that part of the body, and the quality of the voice changes. The spine can become a resonator and even the different parts of the spine—upper, middle, and lower. Sound can be directed to the larynx itself as in Louis Armstrong's way of singing. Once the actor has learned to engage all of these different resonators separately, he can search for the vibration of the entire body. However, as Grotowski and his actors were looking for these different resonators and playing with them in various combinations, the same old problem occurred. The actor's voice began to become strained and mechanical. The actors were putting too much attention on their own instrument and listening to themselves.

Grotowski insisted that an actor should never observe his/her own voice. If an actor, while working, puts his attention on his vocal instrument, he begins to listen to himself. Perhaps he likes what he hears or perhaps he begins to doubt himself. In either case, when he listens to himself, his larynx closes, not entirely, but sort of half-closes. The closure causes him to struggle for fullness and so he begins to force his voice and becomes hoarse. The actor violates the vocal instrument, which can create, after a long period, physiological problems like vocal nodes or chronic laryngitis. Observing one's own vocal instrument and interfering in the organic process must be avoided at each step of working on the voice. As Grotowski and his actors developed different exercises and made various discoveries, they had to remind themselves constantly of this common error. Once the actor begins to observe the instrument, the voice becomes forced and mechanical, the organic process is destroyed, and problems can become aggravated. The way that Grotowski avoided this problem was to work with the actor's echo.

> I observed that if you wanted to create an exterior echo, you could put the resonators in action without any forethought. If you begin to speak toward the ceiling, at this moment, the skull vibrator is going to set itself free by itself. But it must not be a subjective action. The echo should be objective. You must hear the echo. In this case, our attitude, our attention, is not oriented towards ourselves, but towards the outside.
>
> (Grotowski 1971b: 119–20)

So Grotowski began to stimulate the actor from the outside, coaxing him to engage in dialogue with the ceiling (for the occipital resonator), with the wall (for the chest or spine resonator), and with the floor (for the stomach resonator). He looked for different associations of space and animals, relationships and environment. He determined that the voice must always be seeking contact, directed toward a precise place in the space, and listening for feedback, in order to adjust and make new contact.

Exercise 4.9: playing with the voice

Have the actor begin to recite some well-memorized text or sing a song. Often a nursery rhyme from their childhood works well here. While leading the actor around the room, ask her to engage in a dialogue with the ceiling using the text or song, listening for the echo and responding to the echo with the text. It's as if the mouth is on the top of the head. The head is not thrown back, but forward and the actor is truly trying to make contact with the ceiling from the top of the head. Next a dialogue with the wall is improvised. The voice originates in and extends from the chest. "Your mouth is in your chest!" The echo is the answer. It must be heard and reacted to with the whole body. The actor then seeks contact with the floor. "Your mouth is in your stomach! You are like a fat, lazy cow. No, not on all fours. Standing! Let your stomach hang loose. Direct the voice toward the floor between your legs. Listen for the echo! React! Adjust! Make it a conversation, a dialogue!"

The cycle of exercises uses:

- the head voice (toward the ceiling)
- the mouth voice (as if speaking to the air in front of the actor)
- the occipital voice (toward the ceiling behind the actor)
- the chest voice (project toward the wall in front of the actor)
- the stomach voice (toward the floor)
- the shoulder blades (toward the ceiling behind the actor)
- the middle of the spine (toward the wall behind the actor)
- the lumbar region (toward the floor, the wall, and the room behind the actor).

The instructor can stimulate the actor's body by touching or kneading the regions being worked and releasing the impulses that carry the voice.

However, always be careful not to touch in any kind of invasive fashion. The pace of the exercise should be fast. No time for thinking. The whole body (of both the actor and the instructor) must always be engaged and the echo must be caught each time.

Once the resonators have been identified and engaged, a different kind of playing can occur through associations. The game-playing here should engage memories, imagination, relationships with life-partners and actor-partners. "Imagine you are dancing in the warm, spring rain. Sing to the rain. Now lie down on the floor. The sun is beating on your chest. It is warm and spreading across your body. Sing to the sun. Hold yourself like a baby. Rock yourself. Sing a lullaby to yourself. Now sing to your lover. He has put his hand on your head. He is touching your chest." In this way, point by point, the actor's impulses are released and the voice emerges naturally from the body, without forcing, without any artificiality. There should be no screaming or shouting; no automatic repetitions of words or phrases; no planned or choreographed movements. The actor must trust the instructor implicitly and allow herself to be lead into the unknown. And always sing toward the exterior, sing to make contact. Listen for the echo to understand if the contact has been accomplished and then adjust and sing again. It is a clear process. The vocal instrument is an empty channel. Just let the voice pour forth. "Sing to the wall, but farther than this wall. It's a mountain. Sing to the mountain, to someone far away. No, don't shout. Mountain people don't shout! They sing to the abyss. Now there's a bird walking on your left shoulder. Sing for him. And now, the bird is pecking your skull, at the nape of your neck, under the occipital joint. Try to get him to stop by sending vibration there. Sing to make him stop! What was your first pet's name? Sing for her. Sing for Lady." There are many associations that can be used, but they should always be directed toward the space and each should be formulated to set free the impulses of the body-memory. As Grotowski says, "You can't work with the voice without working with the body-memory" (Grotowski 1971b: 124).

The voice can become long and large like a tube or sharp like a sword. Animal and nature images, plants, and fantastic images are all material for setting free the body impulses which carry the voice. The images must be associative and oriented toward a precise direction in the space. This game-playing is intended to liberate the body-memory and extend it in space through the voice. You are always in process and always looking for contact. This work should allow the actor to understand that the voice is not limited and that it can do anything. The impossible is possible. However, Grotowski warns against delving into memories and associations that are too intimate or personal. Only if these intimate confessions open by themselves should they be worked in exercises. The instructor should never provoke such confession. The actor must keep this material for the creative work and be careful not to empty himself during exercises (Grotowski 1971b: 124).

Besides the individual work on the voice, we have developed several exercises to work on the voice as a group. The first of these is called Listening.

Exercise 4.10: Listening

Listening is a structure (similar to Watching) that was created with two objectives: To learn to listen and to work the limits of the voice. The exercise consists of several stages, each with certain rules. The participants must always listen to the others, must work their voice, and must be attentive to the use of the space. A leader who is familiar with the structure can help to signal the passage from one stage to the next. The participants begin by placing themselves in the designated space. They can sit, stand, or lie down. The stages are as follows:

1 Attention to respiration

    a   Begin by listening to the sounds outside the space.

    b   Listen to the sounds around you, in the space.

    c   Listen to your own body's sounds—your breathing, your heartbeat, your digestion and then

2 Wake up the body with vibration (using the sound Ah)

    a   Begin to send vibration to the different parts of your body using the sound ahhh. Make your body vibrate. Take a bath in vibration. This should be a dynamic waking up of the body. Not sluggish. But always listening to the others.

    b   When the body is vibrating, the participant can begin to put her attention to the space and begins to

3 Look for vibration in the space (using the sound Who)

   a The participant transforms the sound from ahh to whoo and
      begins to explore the space to make different vibrations and
      echoes.
   b The participant sends the voice to the floor, to the wall, to the
      various objects in the space, the light fixtures, etc. Trying to
      make each spatial element vibrate and/or echo.
   c After he has explored the space, the participant listens for
      someone else's echo and begins to

4 Connect with a partner (using the sound Why)

   a The partners begin a dialogue. It is a dialogue of vibration.
      It is not a daily-life conversation. It is a simple connection.
      Try to get your partner to move away, to come toward you,
      to turn, to go down, or to come up. Keep it simple at first.
      Work with your whole body. Don't tense the head and
      neck. Send vibration from all of your body. You don't always
      need to have eye contact. Keep moving and listening. Give
      and take.
   b The dialogue is only between two. However, when one group
      connects with another or the dialogue transforms into a trio
      or quartet, we pass onto

5 Harmony (using the sound whee)

   a The group slowly forms a circle and begins to look for har-
      mony by creating chords.
   b The chords transform to

6 Rhythm/Musical Instruments

   a Each participant begins to explore rhythmic possibilities
      within the harmonies by taking on the qualities of a musical
      instrument.
   b As the group works, they slowly move toward

7 Melody

   a The group begins to look for how to create a song from the
      harmony and rhythm. (It is best if the song has been already
      determined before the exercise begins.)
   b Slowly fragments of melody and words appear as

8   The Song is Born

  a   The song should be born slowly. Not already formed. Once the melody is established, the group must sing the song well.

  b   When the song is sung well, in unison. One person can enter the circle and we pass to

9   Solo Improvisation with the song

  a   Like a jazz singer, the person in the circle can begin to improvise with the song while the rest of the group keeps the rhythm, tempo, and melody. Different jazz singers can enter, one at a time. If one or more members of the group join the jazz singer in the center, the circle must disappear and we pass to

10   Group Improvisation with the song

  a   In this stage, the group looks for ways to play in the space together with the song. Different situations can be discovered, games, dances, calls, and responses, as the group plays in the space with the song.

  b   The group must allow the song to lead them into the play. Don't impose. Always listen and respond. Until it evolves into

11   Duets with the song

  a   As the game evolves, the participants connect with a partner and begin to work duets, dialogues with the song.

  b   When the duets come to a finish

12   You and the song in the space

  a   The individual continues a kind of deconstruction of the song in the space.

  b   Until we are left with

13   You and the song in your body

  a   The participant looks for how the song lives in his body. Where does the vibration center itself? Where does the song emerge? The song is reduced to just one phrase or one word, to its essence for the singer.

  b   Until the song becomes once more vibration and the vibration becomes

14 Respiration

    a   The participant listens to the sounds in his own body.

    b   Listens to the sounds in the space.

    c   Listens to the sounds outside.

End of the exercise.

Listening is a complicated exercise. It takes time to learn each stage and explore it by itself before putting them all together. The instructor should feel free in how to introduce the principles of each stage of the exercise. Once it is learned, however, Listening can be a valuable tool to work on essential skills of improvisation and use of the space, while allowing the actor to explore the limits of his/her voice in a safe and creative structure.

Grotowski admitted that in terms of voice work he knew much more about what *not* to do, than what to do. He often said that the best vocal exercise is just to sing. The actor should sing at every opportunity. Sing while driving, while doing the dishes, cleaning the house, or walking to class. Just sing. Working as a group with songs of tradition can be a very stimulating exercise. Grotowski defined songs of tradition as those songs rooted in a particular culture, "formed in a long arc of time and . . . utilized for sacred or ritual purposes . . . as an element of vehicle" (Grotowski 1995: 128). The songs are usually anonymous. Grotowski focused on songs from the Afro-Caribbean tradition. Singing can be an excellent exercise when freed from the restrictive conditions that so many voice teachers place on it and when approached as a tool to challenge the body and to unblock its living impulses.

Exercise 4.11: singing songs of tradition

The songs of tradition can be selected by the group or may be a cycle of songs proposed by the instructor. First, the songs need to be learned. They should be learned by listening, not by reading the notes. Someone who has mastered the song must teach it to the group until the melody is accomplished impeccably. This process, a kind of return to the oral tradition, can be long and tiresome. It involves a lot of repetition and patience. There should be no improvisation with the song at this point. However, melody is only the surface of the song. To sing the song authentically one must discover the vibratory qualities, not just the notes: "the melody is not the same as the vibratory qualities. It is a delicate point, because—to use a metaphor—it's as if the modern man doesn't hear the difference between the sound of a piano and the sound of a violin. The two types of resonance are very different; but the modern man looks just for the melodic line, without catching the differences of resonance" (Grotowski 1995: 127).

Grotowski gives us two clues as to how to look for the vibratory qualities in practice. They both involve meeting the song on a different level than just singing the melody or notes. First, the song of tradition must be met like a person. There is nothing exotic or mysterious in this. As you are singing, encounter the song and the impulses connected to it as "a person." Is the song a woman or a man? A child or an old person? From the hills or the plains? The sea or the river? The valley or the forest? Is it a song of work or play? Or is it a song-animal? A song-force? The contact with a song in this manner allows us to determine the impulses and actions associated with the song. And without turning this into some kind of recipe or method—if the song is well sung (the melody is precise and the vibratory qualities are captured), and the right questions are being asked, then something like the "song-body" can appear. The impulses of life associated with the song (rooted in organicity) run through the body carrying the song. "And then, all of a sudden, the song begins to *sing us*. That ancient song sings me: I don't know anymore if I am finding the song or if I am that song" (Grotowski 1995: 127). The song arrives.

The second clue Grotowski gives us regarding the song of tradition involves looking for the seed of the song. If you ask yourself who was the first singer of this song and how did he/she begin to sing the song, you can find the true beginning of the song, the seed of its vibratory quality. We know that most songs are not composed from beginning to end. Often the kernel, the original singer's impulse to sing the song, lies elsewhere in the song. It is not a question to be answered intellectually or academically, but in the doing. The song becomes a yantra or instrument to discover "first, the corporality of somebody known, and then more and more distant, the corporality of the unknown one, the ancestor. Is this corporality literally as it was? Maybe not literally, but yet as it might have been. You can arrive very far back, as if your memory awoke" (Grotowski 1988: 378–9).

Working with a song in this manner is like stalking the song—and it involves a shift from what might be called **self-consciousness** (related to our identity, our personality, ego, and constructed, social I) to what might be called **self-awareness**. Self-awareness brings attention to structure, to continuity, to basic nature, to the sources from which authentic behavior arises. The separation between body and mind heals. The singer is in a state of atonement (at-one-ment), which includes a softening of the boundaries between person and environment. Alexandra and Roger Pierce describe the experience this way: "The self, rather than being fixed in its context and image of itself, becomes fluid enough to be continually refined and shaped by the experience it generates, to be made new by it in the moment to moment process of living" (Pierce and Pierce 1989: 97–8). Inauthentic or incongruent behavior dissolves. In Grotowski's words, "the body becomes a channel open to the energies, and finds the conjunction between the rigor of elements and the flow of life ('spontaneity')" (Grotowski 1995: 129).

Grotowski warned that this kind of work with songs should not be applied like some kind of method. These are only two examples of the range of possibilities of work on songs of tradition. The group should sing the songs, repeating them until the melody is mastered, and then seek to discover the impulses and actions the songs demand. When this occurs the singer becomes sensitive to the flow of energies and vibrations associated with each song and can begin to use the songs as a tool for work on oneself.

THE ACTOR'S SCORE: TO DO

During his lectures at the Collège de France in 1997, Grotowski stressed again that exercises by themselves do not lead toward the creative act and should never be used as a substitute for work on the role. The objective should always be the creative act. Exercises can serve two purposes in getting there. First, they can aid in stemming the descent into old age. In other words, exercises can keep your instrument in shape and help you "die a little less each day." Second, exercises can unblock certain technical possibilities in the organism. For example, many actors close their larynx when speaking. A blocked larynx prevents the air from carrying the voice and projecting it outward. This often happens when a person is under stress and actors are almost always under stress. So exercises should be developed to unblock the larynx. Grotowski's research into physical and vocal exercises usually originated in his perception of some individual problem or psychophysical block in one of the company's actors. Grotowski was always opposed to any kind of "box of tricks" for the actor. But his actors were adepts in the "laws governing craft." "We are trying to discover those objective laws which govern the expression of an individual" (Grotowski cited in Kumiega 1985: 117). However, how does one make the actor conscious of the elements of his/her craft? What are the creative ways to allow the actor to understand that these laws/elements/tools exist and are at their disposal, need to be applied consciously (at first) in the investigation of resistances, habits, and work on oneself, and should become ingrained in the body (second nature)? The answer lies in getting the actor to understand how to work with action.

Exercise 4.12: The Four Steps

One way in which we try to introduce the novice actor to the possibilities of working with action is with an exercise we call The Four Steps: You have just been cast in a play called The Four Steps. When you get the script all it says is: The actor takes four steps. What do you do? Start working. Take four steps. Make sure each step has a clear beginning, middle, and end. Construct an initial score—for now just movement. Once the movement score is clear, we can begin to transform the movement into action. Let's begin to build the circumstances of our play. Where are you? How does the precise place/space change your four steps and how you execute them? Inside or outside? Humid or dry? Who are you? What age are you? Let's say you are you—but you now, younger, or you older? Who are you with? Or who is watching you? In other words, who is your partner? What are you wearing? Especially, what kind of shoes? How do they make you move differently? When is this taking place? What kind of light? What kind of temperature? How do the light and temperature affect how you accomplish the four steps? Make choices. Keep repeating the four steps. Always being precise with the space. Where you begin, where you end. Don't just do it no matter how. Everything is important. Each moment, each change of weight. Each hesitation and decision. Now you should have your structure more grounded in circumstances. Perhaps it's even connected for you to a precise memory or you have discovered other associations in terms of place or people. How do we continue?

Let's add intention. What are you taking these four steps for? Where are they leading you? Or what are they taking you away from? Be precise.

Make sure you have a clear beginning and ending of each step and of the totality of the action. What changes in the course of these four steps? Do you get what you want? Do you win or lose?

Now let's work technically. What are your eyes doing? How are you looking or seeing at each moment in these four steps? Are you staring? Why? Does your way of looking change? If not, why not? How are you seeing the space? How are you seeing your partner? How does the light affect your way of seeing? How does your way of seeing change with each step?

Now let's imagine that a director arrives. The director begins to add his "concept" to the play. In the middle of the second step, you hear a noise behind you. Repeat. At the beginning of the third step, a bird attacks you and then flies away. No, not during all of the third step, only at the beginning. After the bird flies away you can continue with the middle and end of the third step.

And we continue like this: a new director arrives from the Black Light Theatre of Bullah. He only wants to see hands, so he puts you in white gloves and you must repeat your action with attention to what your hands are doing at each moment. Then another director arrives. He only wants to see feet. Again repeat with attention to the clarity of your feet. And so on... In the end, The Four Steps has become a very interesting and engaging action, full of detail and precisely performed. From Four Steps, we have arrived at a score of physical action performed with intention and precision. This is a very elementary exercise, but it makes the point about how one can begin to work on action from something as simple as a footstep. There is no excuse for not finding action.

An actor can train and do exercises for years without truly attaining a level of competence in the craft of acting. That is why it is necessary to pass to creative work without delay and to find material that can be finely honed in a "non-dilettante, non-touristic" manner. One way to do this is through an **individual action**. In the Grotowski lexicon, these individual actions have also been called individual **ethnodramas** or **mystery plays**.

Exercise 4.13: the individual action

Grotowski recommends starting with an old song. This song should have strong links to your ethno-familial tradition. Perhaps it is the first song you remember your mother or grandfather singing—a lullaby, hymn, or holiday carol. The song should have some quality and not be too banal. "Happy Birthday" or "Rubber Ducky" songs do not work for this exercise. One should approach the song "as if, in it, were codified in potentiality (movement, action, rhythm...) a totality" (Grotowski 1989: 302). The song knows what you should do, how you should perform it. You build a structure around the song. And then you begin to work this structure—in a vertical fashion. Do not build structure after structure, but focus on what you uncover initially, in terms of action and movement, and refine that.

There are several ways to refine an individual action. Once the right song and the story and personal associations that go with the song are discovered, an initial structure is built, and is found to work, then the actor must reconstruct the action in a more condensed form, eliminating anything that is not necessary. "You must rebuild, and rememorize the first proposition (the line of small physical actions), but eliminating all the actions that are not absolutely necessary" (Grotowski 1989: 302). As one begins to edit the line of physical action, various technical problems appear. If you make cuts, how do you rejoin the different fragments?

> For instance, you can apply the following principle: line of physical actions—stop—elimination of a fragment—stop—line of physical actions. Like in cinema, the sequence of movement stops on a fixed image—we cut—another fixed image marks the beginning of a new sequence in movement. This gives: physical action—stop—stop—physical action. But what must be done with the cut, with the hole? At the first stop you are, let's say, standing with your arms up and, at the second stop, sitting with your arms down. One of the solutions consists then in carrying out the passage from one position to the other as a technical demonstration of ability, almost like a ballet, a game of ability. It is only one possibility among others.
>
> (Grotowski 1989: 302–3)

The montage of the vocal score with the physical score is another problem to resolve: Do I sing and move at the same time? When I stop, do I continue to sing? Or do I sing without moving? What's important is that the material is worked coherently and systematically and, although there may be moments of crisis and boredom while working, the action is never allowed to descend into chaos. The elements become more and more condensed and refined. As Grotowski describes it:

> Then, your body must completely absorb all this and recover its organic reactions. You must turn back, toward the seed of the first proposition and find that which, from the point of view of this primary motivation, requires a new restructuring of the whole. So the work does not develop "to the side, to the side" but...always through phases of organicity, of crisis, of organicity, etc. We can say that each phase of spontaneity of life is always followed by a phase of technical absorption.
>
> (Grotowski 1989: 303)

Work on an individual action, gives the actor the opportunity to confront many of the various challenges in constructing a score of physical action and shaping a performance piece, while working on material that is important and connected to one's own roots and sources. The true individual action becomes like a personal prayer for the actor. Something he can go back to again and again in order to remember elements of craft and to reconnect with what is important to him as a performer. The departure point can be the structure or it can be a line of personal associations. It can be something imposed from the exterior (e.g. from a director or a script or text or song) or it can be something which arrives organically from the doer himself.

THE ACTOR'S PARTNER: TO MEET

Contact is one of the essential elements of the performer's work. Nothing can happen without the partner, the other—whether real or invisible. The actor now has the tools to work with space and time and to work on the basic actions of to see and to listen. Now comes the third essential action: to meet. In order to work on contact, Grotowski developed an exercise he called Connection/Disconnection (not to be confused with the Connection/Disconnection stage of the exercise Watching).

Exercise 4.14: Connection/Disconnection

Once an actor has developed his individual action to a level of competence, under the guidance of a director, two individual actions can be put in relation to each other in the space. This is accomplished by selecting moments of connection between the two performers. The moments of connection are fixed in the space through eye contact: Stop—connect—stop—disconnect—continue your score. When the Connection/Disconnections are incorporated into the score and well-rehearsed, a kind of "harmonic improvisation" occurs, "improvisation as readaptation to a structure" (Grotowski 1989: 302). The individual actions are performed in the space, first one then the other and then together with the connections and disconnections. The performers should not attempt to play any kind of new story, but should maintain their original associations and line of action. In this way, for the observer, the point becomes clear how the actor can play one line of actions, tell one story, and the observer can see an entirely different story.

Exercise 4.15: The Rendering

To work on the tools of the actor's craft as a group, in NWPL we have developed an exercise called The Rendering (Figure 4.4). The Rendering is a structured improvisation which may include songs, dances, exercises like Four Corners or Watching, and even individual actions. The director organizes these various elements into an order and the group begins to work on adapting, seeing, listening, and finding the way to create the space and time for the others to do. There is often no story. It is a framework that serves to identify the performer's habitual responses and social masks in order to reclaim his/her vital forces and capacity for contact. As the performer struggles for mastery of the body and voice, vitality and purpose, he/she engages in a process of remembering, revealing, and accomplishing. The Rendering seeks to liberate the dormant energy and creative impulses in the performer, in solitude or in company, with the space or with the partner. The Rendering is an attempt to rediscover the urge to act.

Rendering is a technique that can be used as part of a rehearsal process. It corresponds to Grotowski's work with improvisation and is a slow search for the essential, for actions that are literal.

During The Rendering, the performers should not seek some kind of emotional or psychological self-expression. The goal is to see that life is neither this nor that; it just is. For those doing, The Rendering takes

Figure 4.4 The Rendering. NWPL. Poland (2002). Photograph by Douglas-Scott
    Goheen

place in ecological time, eco-time, not ego time: the interaction of
one's whole being with the reality of here and now. What does it mean
to be alive right now? To refuse numbness and security in favor of
risk and immediacy? In The Rendering there is no place to hide. It
is pure work. And this kind of work is part of the craft tradition; it is
continuous with life.

AFTERWORD

GROTOWSKI'S GIFT

We want to conclude with a brief portrait of Grotowski as a human being. Grotowski was a genuine genius. In writing about his practice and his ethics, his qualities of generosity and humor can sometimes get lost. He was full of life and wit. He had an almost child-like capacity to laugh at the absurdity of existence. He enjoyed good conversation and good cognac. He relished silence and discretion. He could be unrelentingly demanding, but his power was never manipulative or abusive.

Grotowski had the ability to see the kernel of the problem in each situation and in each individual. And not only see the problem, but also propose a creative solution. He never tired of this—what tired him was the other: the way most of us approach a situation, the entropy, the recipes, and the mechanical responses. But to sit next to him as he carefully observed an actor struggle; to brainstorm with him about the next step; to watch him physically transform as he approached the actor with a new task or stimulate him or her with a shout or a whisper was to know someone who worked with compassion—sometimes cruel compassion, but always compassion. And this one might say is even heroic, not in the mythic meaning of the word, but in the sense of doing something that is at once

> necessary and private and extremely difficult, something that requires
> doing the one thing we try to avoid at all costs: to put our whole selves
> into a situation.
>
> (Slowiak 2000a: 30, 2000b: 42–3)

This was Grotowski's gift to us. And this is what we try to remember each day as we approach our own work, our own lives. It has been said that Grotowski's contribution to theatre will be fleeting because he left behind him no tangible body of work to study. But his true legacy will be found in the lives of the people with whom he worked. How each of us carries on his tradition will be the real test of Grotowski's influence—in theatre and beyond theatre.

BIBLIOGRAPHY

BOOKS AND JOURNALS

Banu, Georges (1996) "Grotowski – the Absent Presence," in *Intercultural Performance Reader* (ed.) Patrice Pavis, New York: Routledge.

Barba, Eugenio (1965) "Theatre Laboratory 13 Rzedow," in *The Grotowski Sourcebook* (2001) (eds) Richard Schechner and Lisa Wolford, New York: Routledge, 73–82; first printed in *The Drama Review*, 9, 3:153–71.

—— (1999) *Land of Ashes and Diamonds: My Apprenticeship in Poland, followed by 26 letters from Jerzy Grotowski to Eugenio Barba*, Aberystwyth: Black Mountain Press.

Beckett, Samuel (1984) *Collected Shorter Plays*, New York: Grove Weidenfeld.

Bentley, Eric (1969) "An Open Letter to Grotowski," in *The Grotowski Sourcebook* (2001) (eds) Richard Schechner and Lisa Wolford, New York: Routledge, 165–70; first printed as "Dear Grotowski: An Open Letter," in *The New York Times*, November 30, 1969: 1, 7.

Blonski, Jan (1979) "Holiday or Holiness?: A Critical Reevaluation of Grotowski," trans. Boleslaw Taborski, in *Twentieth Century Polish Theatre* (ed.) Bohdan Drozdowski, trans. Catherine Itzen, London: John Calder; Dallas, TX: Riverrun Press.

Braun, Edward (1982) *The Director and the Stage: From Naturalism to Grotowski*, London: Methuen; New York: Holmes & Meyer.

Braun, Kazimierz (1996) *A History of Polish Theater, 1939–1989: Spheres of Captivity and Freedom*, London, Westport, CT: Greenwood Press.

Brecht, Stefan (1970) "The Laboratory Theatre in New York, 1969: A Set of Critiques," in *The Grotowski Sourcebook* (2001) (eds) Richard Schechner and Lisa Wolford, New York: Routledge, 118–33; first printed in *The Drama Review*, 14, 2: 178–211.

Brook, Peter (1968a) *The Empty Space*, London: McGibbon & Kee; New York: Atheneum.

—— (1968b) "Preface," in Jerzy Grotowski, *Towards a Poor Theatre* (2002) (ed.) Eugenio Barba, New York: Routledge, 11–13; first published New York: Simon and Schuster, 1968.

—— (1995) "Grotowski, Art as Vehicle," in *The Grotowski Sourcebook* (2001) (eds) Richard Schechner and Lisa Wolford, New York: Routledge, 381–4.

Burzynski, Tadeusz and Osinski, Zbigniew (1979) *Grotowski's Laboratory*, trans. Boleslaw Taborski, Warsaw: Interpress.

Cioffi, Kathleen (1996) *Alternative Theatre in Poland 1954–1989*, Amsterdam: Harwood Academic Publishers.

Croyden, Margaret (1969) "Notes from the Temple: A Grotowski Seminar," in *The Drama Review*, 14, 1, Fall: 178–83.

—— (1993) *In the Shadow of the Flame: Three Journeys*, New York: Continuum.

Cuesta, Jairo (2000) "On His Way," in *Slavic and East European Performance*, 20, 2, Summer: 26–7.

—— (2003a) "Sentieri verso il Cuore: In forma di contesto," in *Culture Teatrali*, 9, Autumn: 25–30.

—— (2003b) "Ritorno alle 'Sorgenti', in *Culture Teatrali*," 9, Autumn: 31–6.

Czerwinski, Edward J. (1988) *Contemporary Polish Theatre and Drama (1956–1984)*, New York: Greenwood Press.

Eckhart, Meister (1991) *Breakthrough: Meister Eckhart's Creation Spirituality in New Translation/Introduction and Commentaries by Matthew Fox*, New York: Image Books.

Findlay, Robert (1980) "Grotowski's 'Cultural Explorations Bordering on Art, Especially Theatre'," *Theatre Journal*, 32, 3, October: 349–56.

—— (1984) "Grotowski's *Akropolis*: A Retrospective View," in *Modern Drama*, 27, 1, March: 1–20.

—— (1986) "Grotowski's Laboratory Theatre: Dissolution and Diaspora," reprinted and revised in *The Grotowski Sourcebook* (2001) (eds) Richard Schechner and Lisa Wolford, New York: Routledge, 172–88; first printed in *The Drama Review* 30, 3: 201–25.

Flaszen, Ludwik (1965) "Akropolis: Treatment of the Text," trans. Simone Sanzenbach in Jerzy Grotowski *Towards a Poor Theatre* (2002), New York: Routledge, 61–77.

Flaszen, Ludwik and Grotowski, Jerzy (2001) *Il Teatr Laboratorium di Jerzy Grotowski 1959–1969* (eds) Ludwik Flaszen and Carla Pollastrelli, Pontedera, Italy: Fondazione Pontedera Teatro.

Grimes, Ronald L. (1981) "The Theatre of Sources," in *The Grotowski Sourcebook* (2001) (eds) Richard Schechner and Lisa Wolford, New York: Routledge, 271–80; first printed in *TDR: A Journal of Performance Studies*, 35, 3: 67–74.

—— (1982) *Beginnings in Ritual Studies*, Landham: University Press of America; 2nd expanded edition: Columbia, SC: University of South Carolina Press.

Grotowski, Jerzy (1965) "Towards a Poor Theatre," trans. T.K. Wiewiorowski in *The Grotowski Sourcebook* (2001) (eds) Richard Schechner and Lisa Wolford, New York: Routledge, 28–37; first published in *Odra*, volume 9, Wroclaw, 1965; English translation first published in *Tulane Drama Review*, 35, New Orleans, 1967.

—— (1971a) "Les Exercises," in *Action Culturelle du Sud-Est*, supplement 6, 1–13; "Esercizi," in *Sipario*, 104, 1, 1980; in *Il Teatr Laboratorium di Jerzy Grotowski 1959–1969* (2001) (eds) Ludwik Flaszen and Carla Pollastrelli, Pontedera, Italy : Fondazione Pontedera Teatro, 184–204; unpublished translation from French and Italian by James Slowiak.

Grotowski, Jerzy (1971b) "La Voix," in *Le Theatre*, 1: 87–131; "La Voce," in *Il Teatr Laboratorium di Jerzy Grotowski 1959–1969* (2001) (eds) Ludwik Flaszen and Carla Pollastrelli, Pontedera, Italy: Fondazione Pontedera Teatro, 154–183; unpublished translation from French by James Slowiak.

—— (1973) "Holiday: The day that is holy," trans. Boleslaw Taborski, *The Drama Review*, 17, 2(T58), June 1973: 113–35.

—— (1974) "Ce qui fut," in *"jour saint" et autres textes*, Paris: Gallimard, 43–72.

—— (1975) "Conversation with Grotowski," interview with Andrzej Bonarski, in Jennifer Kumiega, *The Theatre of Grotowski*, London, New York: Methuen, 217–23. Text published in abridged version.

—— (1979) "Action is Literal," in Jennifer Kumiega, *The Theatre of Grotowski*, London, New York: Methuen, 224–8. Text published in abridged version.

—— (1982) *Tecniche originarie dell'attore*, Rome: Istituto del Teatro e dello Spettacolo, Universita di Roma.

—— (1988) "Performer," in *The Grotowski Sourcebook* (2001) (eds) Richard Schechner and Lisa Wolford, New York: Routledge, 376–80.

—— (1989) "*Tu es le fils de quelqu'un* [You are someone's son]," English version revised by Jerzy Grotowski, trans. James Slowiak, in *The Grotowski Sourcebook* (2001) (eds) Richard Schechner and Lisa Wolford, New York: Routledge, 294–305.

—— (1995) "From the Theatre Company to Art as Vehicle," in Thomas Richards, *At Work with Grotowski on Physical Actions* (1995), London: Routledge, 115–35.

—— (1996a) "A Kind of Volcano," trans. Magda Złotowska, in Jacob Needleman and George Baker, *Gurdjieff: Essays and Reflections on the Man and His Teaching*, New York: Continuum, 87–106.

—— (1996b) "Orient/Occident," trans. Maureen Schaeffer Price, in *The Intercultural Performance Reader* (ed.) Patrice Pavis, New York and London: Routledge.

—— (1997a) "Holiday [Swieto]: The day that is holy," (revised version) in *The Grotowski Sourcebook* (2001) (eds) Richard Schechner and Lisa Wolford, New York: Routledge, 215–25.

—— (1997b) "Theatre of Sources," in *The Grotowski Sourcebook* (2001) (eds) Richard Schechner and Lisa Wolford, New York: Routledge, 252–70.

—— (1999) "Untitled Text by Jerzy Grotowski, Signed in Pontedera, Italy, July 4, 1998," in *The Drama Review* 43, 2(T162), Summer 1999: 11–12.

—— (2002) *Towards a Poor Theatre* (ed.) Eugenio Barba, New York: Routledge; first published New York: Simon and Schuster, 1968.

Harrop, John and Epstein, Sabin R. (1982) *Acting With Style*, Englewood Cliffs, NJ: Prentice Hall.

Hillman, James (1996) *The Soul's Code*, New York: Random House.

Innes, Christopher (1981) *Holy Theatre: Ritual and the Avant Garde*, Cambridge: Cambridge University Press.

—— (1993) *Avant Garde Theatre, 1892–1992*, New York: Routledge.

Kahn, Francois (1997) *The Vigil [Czuwanie]* trans. Lisa Wolford, in *The Grotowski Sourcebook* (2001) (eds) Richard Schechner and Lisa Wolford, New York: Routledge, 226–30.

Kolankiewicz, Leszek (ed.) (1978) *On the Road to Active Culture: The Activities of Grotowski's Theatre Laboratory Institute in the Years 1970–1977*, Wroclaw: Instytut Aktora-Teatr Laboratorium.

Kott, Jan (1984) *The Theater of Essence and Other Essays*, Evanston: Northwestern University Press.

—— (1992) *Memory of the Body*, Evanston, IL: Northwestern University Press.

Kumiega, Jennifer (1978) "Grotowski/The Mountain Project," in *The Grotowski Sourcebook* (2001) (eds) Richard Schechner and Lisa Wolford, New York: Routledge, 231–47; first printed *Dartington Theatre Papers*, series 2, number 9, Dartington Hall.

—— (1985) *The Theatre of Grotowski*, London, New York: Methuen.

Lendra, I. Wayan (1991) "The Motions: A detailed description," in *The Drama Review*, 35, 1: 129–38.

Martin, Jacqueline (1991) *Voice in Modern Theatre*, New York: Routledge.

Mennen, Richard (1975) "Grotowski's Paratheatrical Projects," *TDR: A Journal of Performance Studies*, 19, 4, December: 58–69.

Milling, Jane and Ley, Graham (2001) *Modern Theories of Performance: From Stanislavsky to Boal*, Hampshire: Palgrave.

Mindell, Arnold (1982) *Dreambody: The Body's Role in Revealing the Self*, Boston, MA: Sigo Press.

Mitter, Shomit (1992) *Systems of Rehearsal: Stanislavsky, Brecht, Grotowski and Brook*, New York: Routledge.

Needleman, Jacob and George Baker (eds) (1996) *Gurdjieff: Essays and Reflections on the Man and His Teaching*, New York: Continuum.

Newham, Paul (1994) *The Singing Cure: An Introduction to Voice Movement Therapy*, Boston, MA: Shambhala.

Ortega y Gasset, José (1972) *Meditations on Hunting*, New York: Scribner.

Osinski, Zbigniew (1986) *Grotowski and His Laboratory*, trans. and abridged by Lillian Vallee and Robert Findlay, New York: PAJ Publications.

—— (1991) "Grotowski Blazes the Trails," in *The Grotowski Sourcebook* (2001) (eds) Richard Schechner and Lisa Wolford, New York: Routledge, 385–400; first printed in *The Drama Review*, 35, 1: 95–112.

Pierce, Alexandra and Pierce, Roger (1989) *Expressive Movement: Posture and Action in Daily Life, Sports, and the Performing Arts*, New York: Plenum Press.

Reymond, Lizelle (1995) *To Live Within*, Portland, OR: Rudra Press.

Richards, Thomas (1995) *At Work with Grotowski on Physical Actions*, London, New York: Routledge.

—— (1997) *The Edge-point of Performance*, an interview with Thomas Richards by Lisa Wolford, Pontedera, Italy: Documentation Series of the Workcenter of Jerzy Grotowski.

Rilke, Rainer Maria (1986) *Rodin and Other Prose Pieces*, London: Quartet Books.

Ronen, Dan (1978) "A Workshop with Ryszard Cieslak," *TDR: A Journal of Performance Studies*, 22, 4, December: 67–76.

Roose-Evans, James (1989) *Experimental Theatre*, New York: Routledge.

Rudakova, Irina (1999) " 'Action is Literal': Ritual Typology and 'Ritual Arts'," in *Theatre and Holy Script* (ed.) Shimon Levy, Brighton, Portland, OR: Sussex Academic Press.

Schechner, Richard (1985) *Between Theater and Anthropology*, Philadelphia, PA: University of Philadelphia Press.

—— (1988) *Performance Theory*, revised and expanded ed., London, New York: Routledge.

—— (1993) *The Future of Ritual*, New York: Routledge.

Schechner, Richard and Wolford, Lisa (eds) (2001) *The Grotowski Sourcebook*, London, New York: Routledge; first published 1997.

Schneider, Rebecca and Cody, Gabrielle (2001) *Re-Direction: A Theoretical and Practical Guide*, New York: Routledge.

Shawn, Wallace and Gregory, André (1981) *My Dinner with André*, New York: Grove Press.

Slowiak, James (2000a) "Grotowski: The Teacher," in *Slavic and East European Performance*, 20, 2, Summer: 28–30.

—— (2000b) "Ondas en el estanque [Ripples in the Pond] trans. Carlota Llano in *Grotowski: Testimonios* (ed.) Fernando Montes, Bogota: Ministerio de Cultura de Colombia, 34–43.

Smith, Michael (1969) *Theatre Trip*, Indianapolis, New York: Bobbs-Merrill Company.

TDR: A Journal of Performance Studies (1991) (ed.) Richard Schechner, 35, 1: whole issue.

Taviani, Ferdinando (1992) "In Memory of Ryszard Cieslak," in *The Grotowski Sourcebook* (2001) (eds) Richard Schechner and Lisa Wolfrord, New York: Routledge, 189–204.

Temkine, Raymonde (1972) *Grotowski*, New York: Avon Books.

Turner, Victor (1982) *From Ritual to Theatre: The Human Seriousness of Play*, New York: PAJ Publications.

Turner, Victor (1986) *The Anthropology of Performance*, New York: PAJ Publications.

Wangh, Stephen (2000) *An Acrobat of the Heart: A Physical Approach to Acting Inspired by the Work of Jerzy Grotowski*, with an afterword by André Gregory, New York: Vintage Books.

Wiles, Timothy (1980) *The Theater Event: Modern Theories of Performance*, Chicago, IL: University of Chicago Press.

Wolford, Lisa (1994) "Re/Membering Home and Heritage: The New World Performance Laboratory," *TDR: A Journal of Performance Studies*, 38, 3: 128–51.

—— (1995) "Approaching Grotowski's Work-Without-Witness," *Slavic and East European Performance*, 15, 3, Fall: 16–25.

—— (1996a) *Grotowski's Objective Drama Research*, Jackson, MS: University Press of Mississippi.

—— (1996b) "Action: The Unrepresentable Origin," in *The Grotowski Sourcebook* (2001) (eds) Richard Schechner and Lisa Wolford, New York: Routledge, 409–26; first printed in *TDR: A Journal of Performance Studies*, 40, 4, Winter: 134–53.

—— (1996c) "*Ta-wil* of Action: The New World Performance Laboratory's Persian Cycle," *New Theatre Quarterly*, 46: 156–76.

—— (1998) "Grotowski's Art as Vehicle: The Invention of an Esoteric Tradition," *Performance Research*, 3, 3, Winter: 85–95.

—— (2000) "Grotowski's Vision of the Actor: The Search for Contact," in *Twentieth Century Actor Training* (ed.) Alison Hodge, London, New York: Routledge.

—— (2001) "Ambivalent Positionings: Grotowski's Art as Vehicle and the Paradox of Categorization," in *Performer Training: Developments Across Cultures* (ed.) Ian Watson, Amsterdam: Harwood Academic Publishers.

Workcenter of Jerzy Grotowski (1988) Pontedera, Italy: Centro per le sperimentazione e la ricerca teatrale.

VIDEO

Akropolis (1971) directed by James MacTaggart, produced by Lewis Freedman, New York: Arthur Cantor, Inc.

Jerzy Grotowski (1997) directed and produced by Merrill Brockway, Kent, CT: Creative Arts Television Archive.

My Dinner with André (1981) directed by Louis Malle, produced by George W. George and Beverly Karp, New York: Fox Lorber Home Video.

Training at the "Teatr Laboratorium" in Wroclaw (1972) directed by Torgeir Wethal, Holstebro, Denmark: Odin Teatret Film.

AUDIO TAPES

Grotowski, Jerzy (1997c) *Anthropologie théâtrale*. Inaugural lesson for Collège de France at Théâtre des Bouffes du Nord, March 24, 1997, Paris: Le Livre qui parle.

—— (1997d, 1998) *La lignée organique au théâtre et dans le rituel*. Series of seminars for Collège de France, October 6, 13, 20, June 2, 16, 23, 1997 and January 12, 26, 1998, Paris: Le livre qui parle (14 cassettes).

USEFUL WEBSITES

www.tracingroadsacross.net

www.grotcenter.art.pl

www.nwplab.org

INDEX

Related titles from Routledge

The Routledge Companion to Theatre and Performance

Edited by Paul Allain and Jen Harvie

What is theatre? What is performance? What are their connections and differences? What events, people, practices and ideas have shaped theatre and performance in the twentieth century, and, importantly, where are they heading next?

Proposing answers to these big questions, *The Routledge Companion to Theatre and Performance* provides an informative and engaging introduction to the significant people, events, concepts and practices that have defined the complementary fields of theatre and performance studies.

Including over 120 entries in three easy-to-use, alphabetical sections, this fascinating text presents a wide range of individuals and topics, from performance artist Marina Abramovic, to directors Vsevolod Meyerhold and Robert Wilson, The Living Theatre's *Paradise Now, the haka*, multimedia performance, political protest and visual theatre.

With each entry containing crucial historical and contextual information, extensive cross-referencing, detailed analysis, and an annotated bibliography, *The Routledge Companion to Theatre and Performance* is undoubtedly a perfect reference guide for the keen student and passionate theatre-goer alike.

ISBN Hb: 978–0–415–25720–6
ISBN Pb: 978–0–415–25721–3

**Available at all good bookshops
For ordering and further information please visit:
www.routledge.com**

Related titles from Routledge

Performance Studies: An Introduction
2nd Edition
Richard Schechner

Praise for the first edition:
'An appropriately broad-ranging, challenging, and provocative
introduction, equally important for practicing artists as for students and
scholars of the performing arts.'

- Phillip Zarrilli, *University of Exeter*

Fully revised and updated in light of recent world events, this important
new edition of a key introductory textbook by a prime mover in the field
provides a lively and accessible overview of the full range of performance.

Performance Studies includes discussion of the performing arts and popular
entertainments, rituals, play and games as well as the performances of
every day life. Supporting examples and ideas are drawn from the
performing arts, anthropology, post-structuralism, ritual theory, ethology,
philosophy and aesthetics.

The text has been fully revised, with input from leading teachers and trialled
with students. User-friendly, with a special text design, it also includes:

- new examples, biographies, source material and photographs
- numerous extracts from primary sources giving alternative voices
  and viewpoints
- biographies of key thinkers
- activities to stimulate fieldwork, classroom exercises and discussion
- key readings for each chapter
- twenty line drawings and 202 photographs drawn from private and
  public collections around the world.

For undergraduates at all levels and beginning graduate students in performance studies, theatre, performing arts and cultural studies, this is the
must-have book in the field.

Hb: 978–0–415–37245–9
Pb: 978–0–415–37246–6

Available at all good bookshops
For ordering and further information please visit:
www.routledge.com

Related titles from Routledge

The Performance Studies Reader
Edited by Henry Bial

'A collection of this type has been needed for a long time.'

Sally Harrison-Pepper, *Miami University*

'Clearly an important collection of essays that will provide an excellent resource for levels II and III specialist courses.'

Nick Kaye, *Exeter University*

The Performance Studies Reader is a lively and much-needed anthology of critical writings on the burgeoning discipline of performance studies. It provides an overview of the full range of performance theory for undergraduates at all levels, and beginning graduate students in performance studies, theatre, performing arts and cultural studies.

The collection is designed as a companion to Richard Schechner's popular *Performance Studies: an Introduction* but is also ideal as a stand-alone text. Henry Bial collects together key critical pieces from the field, referred to as 'suggested readings' in *Performance Studies: an Introduction*. He also broadens the discussion with additional selections. Featuring contributions from major scholars and artists such as Richard Schechner, Eugenio Barba, Marvin Carlson, Judith Butler, Jon McKenzie, Homi K. Bhabha, Eve Kosofsky Sedgwick and Jerzy Grotowski, this important collection offers a wide-ranging introduction to the main areas of study.

Hb: 978–0–415–30240–1
Pb: 978–0–415–30241–8

**Available at all good bookshops
For ordering and further information please visit:
www.routledge.com**

Related titles from Routledge

Twentieth Century Theatre:
A Sourcebook
Edited by Richard Drain

Twentieth Century Theatre: A Sourcebook is an inspired handbook of ideas
and arguments on theatre. Richard Drain gathers together a uniquely
wide-ranging selection of original writings on theatre by its most creative
practitioners - directors, playwrights, performers and designers, from
Jarry to Grotowski and Craig. These key texts span the twentieth century,
from the onset of modernism to the present, providing direct access to
the thinking behind much of the most stimulating theatre the century
has had to offer, as well as guidelines to its present most adventurous
developments.

Setting theory beside practice, these writings bring alive a number of vital
and continuing concerns, each of which is given full scope in five sections
which explore the Modernist, Political, Inner and Global dimensions of
twentieth century theatre. *Twentieth Century Theatre: A Sourcebook* provides
illuminationg perspectives on past history, and throws fresh light on the
sources and development of theatre today. This sourcebook is not only an
essential and versatile collection for students at all levels, but also directed
numerous devised shows which have toured to theatres, schools,
community centres and prisons.

Hb: 978–0–415–09619–5
Pb: 978–0–415–09620–1